THE BIG GREEN POETRY MACHINE

Poetic Voices

Edited By Briony Kearney

First published in Great Britain in 2023 by:

Young Writers
Remus House
Coltsfoot Drive
Peterborough
PE2 9BF
Telephone: 01733 890066
Website: www.youngwriters.co.uk

All Rights Reserved
Book Design by Ashley Janson
© Copyright Contributors 2023
Softback ISBN 978-1-80459-552-7

Printed and bound in the UK by BookPrintingUK
Website: www.bookprintinguk.com
YB0543Y

FOREWORD

Welcome Reader,

For Young Writers' latest competition The Big Green Poetry Machine, we asked primary school pupils to craft a poem about the world. From nature and environmental issues to exploring their own habitats or those of others around the globe, it provided pupils with the opportunity to share their thoughts and feelings about the world around them.

Here at Young Writers our aim is to encourage creativity in children and to inspire a love of the written word, so it's great to get such an amazing response, with some absolutely fantastic poems. It's important for children to be aware of the world around them and some of the issues we face, but also to celebrate what makes it great! This competition allowed them to express their hopes and fears or simply write about their favourite things. The Big Green Poetry Machine gave them the power of words and the result is a wonderful collection of inspirational and moving poems in a variety of poetic styles.

I'd like to congratulate all the young poets in this anthology; I hope this inspires them to continue with their creative writing.

CONTENTS

Abbey Gate College Infant & Junior School, Aldford

Sammy Thwaites (7)	1
Spencer Howey (8)	2
Abigail Shone-Ward (9)	3
Claudia Leach (8)	4
Maddie Kitchen (11)	5
Thaddy Caustin (8)	6
Isla Ward (9)	7
Charlotte Lee (7)	8
Evie James (7)	9
Lydia Barnes (6)	10
Archie Chantler (7)	11
Nerea Morente Lopez (7)	12
Bertie Chantler (5)	13
Beatrice Bennette (5)	14

Dacre Braithwaite CE (VA) Primary School, Harrogate

Phoebe Adams (10)	15
Scarlett Hotham (10)	16
Logan Moore (11)	18
Josh Phillips (11)	20
Joe Peachey (10)	21
Georgie Gill (9)	22
Rosie Newcomb (10)	24
Reece Sharples (11)	25
Lulu Broadley (11)	26
Mekhi Machama (9)	28
Carter Sunderland (10)	29
Annalise Robinson (9)	30
Jasmine Sharples (11)	31
Alex Randall De Andres (11)	32
Keira Spence (11)	33

Naomi Gray (10)	34
Max Parker (9)	35
Ilse Clawson (9)	36
Faye Braithwaite (10)	37
Hannah Ryder (11)	38
Oliver Marshall (10)	39
Arthur Jackson (9)	40
Lauren Elaine Dobson (9)	41
Charlie Scruton (8)	42
Sam Peachey (8)	43
Ben Marshall (8)	44
Bruno Broadley (8)	45
Alan Ryder (8)	46

Junior King's School, Sturry

Lewis Riggs	47
Edie Wise (10)	48
Felix Zeng (10)	50
Tofarati Oluyemi (10)	52
Benedict Southgate (9)	54
Santiago Chávez Leroy (10)	55
Can Tenteoglu	56
Melody Caruana (10)	57
Jessica Kemp (10)	58
Zen Higson	60
Andrea-Marie Rogivue (9)	61
Charlie s'Jacob (9)	62
Sacha Dhar (9)	63
Lucinda Lapthorn (10)	64
Marina Piccinin (10)	65
Dylan Nish Patel (11)	66
Arthur Norris	67
Vera Kuznetsova (10)	68
Rafe Parle (10)	69
Isabel Chang	70

Harry Cleaver (9) — 71

Markethill Primary School, Armagh

Sophie McNiece (10) — 72
Charlotte Abraham (11) — 74
Chloe McMullan (11) — 76
Samuel Hamilton (10) — 78
Grace Curry (10) — 79
James Barnard (11) — 80
Imogen Henry (11) — 81
Leah Wilson (10) — 82
Zosia Cimochowska (11) — 83
Chloe Callender (11) — 84
Maddison Hill (11) — 86
Eadie Downard (11) — 87
Alice McConnell (10) — 88
Daniel Coalter (11) — 89
Alfie Hartley (10) — 90
Anna McMullan (10) — 91
Sophie Gillow (10) — 92
Harry Black (11) — 93
Joy Dixon (11) — 94
Evie McMullan (10) — 95
Zoe Shaw (10) — 96
Jackson Clarke (10) — 97
Henry McCrum (10) — 98
Mary — 99

St Gabriel's CE Academy, Houlton

Bella Keegan-Devey (10) — 100
Grace Bunker (11) — 102
Maya Arun (10) — 104
Izzy Keegan-Devey (10) — 106
Izzy Campbell-Smyth (11) — 107
Gerrard Headland (9) — 108
Alex Holbrook (8) — 109
Blossom Kanu (11) — 110
Simisola Taiwo (11) — 111
Mithra Seluakumar (8) — 112
Ella-Rose Jaboro (11) — 113
William Darby (11) — 114
Gadi Kamga (5) — 115
Sophia Wood (10) — 116
Romola Taiwo (7) — 117
Edward Arnold (9) — 118
Anaya Khalsa (6) — 119
Colene Twum Ameyaw (11) — 120
Adley Ball (11) — 121
Rae Phillips (5) — 122
Riley O'Leary (11) — 123
Asa Jenner (9) — 124
Reevan Gill (9) — 125
Tymon Orbik (10) — 126
Brooklyn Forrest (6) — 127
Varun Premkumar (7) — 128
Leo Dixon (9) — 129
Georgia Nicholls (7) — 130
Poppy Small-Mercier (9) — 131
Alice Nuttall (7) — 132
Mivaan Gupta (5) — 133
Eliana Prasannakumar (6) — 134
Krishna Pathak (6) — 135
Lauren Smith (10) — 136
Tosia Surowiecka (5) — 137
Jack Kallmeier (6) — 138
Ariyan Gill (9) — 139
Isobel Foster (6) — 140
Kinza Razaq (5) — 141
Sofia Grievson-Alvarez (5) — 142
Mia Hunjan (6) — 143
Jiyanshi Shah (6) — 144
Anudhya Arroju (5) — 145
Aidan Parry (7) — 146
Betsy Makinson (9) — 147
Neeva Valand (6) — 148
Benjamin Pitham (11) — 149
Autumn Griffiths (7) — 150
Erin Dixon (6) — 151
Isaac Beckett (5) — 152
Meredith Neal (6) — 153
Sophia Lupu (5) — 154
Elisha Gospel (6) — 155
Ashira Muppidi (6) — 156
Bobbi-Leigh Grimsley (7) — 157

Name	Page
Heath Norton-Carrington (7)	158
Charlotte Mitchell (10)	159
Archa Sajith (8)	160
Nathan Wilkinson (5)	161
Deacon Marshall (11)	162
Orlaith Wallace (5)	163
Emily Lay (8)	164
Primrose Restall (5)	165
Jake Howard (7)	166
Lucie Lee (8)	167
Lucas Shotton (7)	168
Aleksander Pooley (7)	169
Poppy Hemphill (7)	170
Eeshaan Janapareddy (6)	171
Esther Ikuomola (9)	172
Harriet Scammell (6)	173
Franco James (6)	174
Luna Baulch (5)	175
Hannah Goodship (10)	176
Sam Huddlestone (7)	177
Callan Stead (5)	178
Zara Kanu (9)	179
Esther Lay (8)	180
Faizan Nafiz (5)	181
Poppy Munnings (6)	182
Sullivan Wedge (5)	183
Nash, Sing Hong Li (5), Alfie Howard (5) & Oscar	184
Arya Shaikh (5)	185
Lucy Franklin (6)	186
Kishan Ram (6)	187
Vihaan Reddy Marri (6)	188
Sophie Shotton (5)	189
Edwin Tuton (6)	190
Jonah Cation (9)	191
Aahan David (10)	192
Siddhant Shreyas (10)	193
Josiah Uhiara (5)	194
Cassian Gregg (8)	195
Ellie Chrysakis (8)	196
Logan Gegembauer (6)	197
Edith Whitley (6)	198
Emilia Haggerwood (7)	199
Michael Perrier (8)	200
Lucia Mary Keeley (5)	201
Olivia Miller (6)	202
Antonia Haggerwood (7)	203
Isabella Petit (7)	204
Iris Harrison (7)	205
Imaiya Shaker (8)	206
Harrison Ellard (6)	207
Olivia Rossouw (10)	208
Mollie Puwar (8)	209
Lyra Tailby-Corcoran (6)	210
Caiden Cajic (9)	211
Arielle Shotade (8)	212
Avishai Muppidi (9)	213
Lincoln Baulch (7)	214
Yela Talla Kuate (10)	215
Emily Mitchell (8)	216
Daniel Campbell-Smyth (7)	217
Deepshika Gangadhari (9)	218
David Bogdan (10)	219
Darcie Wallace (8)	220
George Hillsdon-Crook (9)	221
Reha Rachaputi (9)	222
Jaya Sunner (7)	223
Alfred Munnings (9)	224
Prakash Singh (8)	225
Dillon Harris (10)	226
Evelyn Scammell (9)	227
Bentley Ball (8)	228
Lola Wedge (10)	229
Samarth Sriram (10)	230
Seungjoon Kwak (9)	231
Nathan Gunda (10)	232
Amelia Arnold (7)	233
Jaden Kai Tobias Levy (10)	234
Eric Gegembauer (9)	235
Esmé Beneké-Orr (7)	236
Myles Whitley (8)	237
Lottie Clack (9)	238
Mia Sunner (10)	239
Katelin McCormick (9)	240
Olivia Ridley (9)	241
Amelija Tadaraviciute (7)	242

James Chute (9)	243
Ellie Elder (10)	244
William Elliott (9)	245
Aryan Razaq (8)	246
Alva Wedge (8)	247
Lemuel Osei (8)	248
Frank Tuton (8)	249

Warcop CE Primary School, Warcop

Zaki Shihadah (9)	250
Jessica Murray (9)	251
Blake Harbage (9)	252
Abbie Hauser (8)	253
Joseph Harrison (10)	254
Evie Heron (8)	255
Reid Mchale (8)	256
Jessie Mary Heron (9)	257
Charlie Gregg (9)	258
Torrin Baker (8)	259
Georgia Lucy Patterson (9)	260
Fraser Hogg (8)	261

THE POEMS

Save Our Earth

We're going to talk about the climate,
Let's start by saying you're a primate,
There are other primates just like chimps,
And there's oceans full of fish and shrimps,
If the ocean gets too warm,
It will cause a giant storm,
If we keep killing fish,
There'll be no salmon on our dish,
If we kill the ocean blue,
Then all will die, including you,
Cutting down flowers and trees,
Will leave no place left for the bees,
If we stop using so much plastic,
Then our Earth will be fantastic,
If you stop shooting pheasants,
Then our planet's happiness will be your present,
If vulnerable animals keep getting shot,
Then their species will be forgot,
And we shall miss them such a lot.

Sammy Thwaites (7)
Abbey Gate College Infant & Junior School, Aldford

The Big Planet Earth

Hello, children, I am a tree
That has been on Planet Earth for a long time,
I was perfect before,
But then smoke was in the air,
And plastic right next to my roots,
Men were chopping tall trees for their wood,
So I'm going to tell you how to protect the Earth:
Make sure you put stuff in the bin,
Do not use too much electricity,
Because they use oil and that is really bad,
You need to use solar power more,
To get solar power, get a solar panel,
Tell friends about pollution,
And how to stop pollution,
Pollution is going to ruin our future.

Spencer Howey (8)
Abbey Gate College Infant & Junior School, Aldford

Saving Earth

We need to save our Earth,
Because the amount of plastic that is in our oceans, rivers, lakes, and roads
Is silly really,
Because we have bins everywhere,
We shouldn't be throwing it where it does not belong.
So imagine you were an animal,
Or you were a sea creature,
And you saw some plastic and you ate it,
And it got stuck and you could not breathe,
And that is a problem.
Climate change,
Our planet is getting too hot!
Because the gas is going into our ozone layer,
And melting our ice,
So think about what is going to help our planet.

Abigail Shone-Ward (9)
Abbey Gate College Infant & Junior School, Aldford

Save The Animals

Why should we save the bees?
The reason why we should is,
There would be more plants,
And then there would be more honey,
And our future depends on the bees.

Why should we stop global warming?
The reason why we should is,
The North and South Pole ice is melting,
And it is a problem for the animals that live there,
And the water will go higher,
And it will kill animals.

Why should we stop chopping down the trees?
The reason why we should is,
There are no more trees,
We will die,
And some animals live in them.

Claudia Leach (8)
Abbey Gate College Infant & Junior School, Aldford

I Dream

I dream every day of luscious grass and trees taller than a skyscraper,
I dream every day of millions of stars in the night sky, shining beautifully for the eye to see,
I dream every day for God to send angels down from the sky to protect our planet,
I dream every day of mountains to grow from the ground and be as high as the clouds,
My hope, not a dream, is that our world becomes what it used to be.

Maddie Kitchen (11)
Abbey Gate College Infant & Junior School, Aldford

Seasons

Spring,
Blossom everywhere,
The world bouncing out of bed,
Songs dancing on air.

Summer,
Animals learning
The laws of food and living,
On endless hot days.

Autumn,
Under burning trees,
Squirrels bury hopes,
Farmers pick fruits of the sun.

Winter,
Leaves become black boats
Docking on icy islands,
In pearl-dripped green seas.

Thaddy Caustin (8)
Abbey Gate College Infant & Junior School, Aldford

I Have A Dream

I have a dream that in the future,
The world will be a better place.
I have a dream that if we protect our wildlife,
There will be no more extinctions.
I have a dream that if we recycle,
We could change our environment.
I have a dream that if we do good deeds to help our planet,
We can live happier.
I have a dream that, one day,
Our world will be perfect!

Isla Ward (9)
Abbey Gate College Infant & Junior School, Aldford

Saving The Environment

You need to listen and listen well,
I have an important story to tell,
We need to be careful and look after our world,
Can you believe 6.5 million tons of food gets wasted?
You must not throw away your food in haste!
Look after our planet,
The flowers and the trees,
And please, please remember
To listen to me!

Charlotte Lee (7)
Abbey Gate College Infant & Junior School, Aldford

My World

Listen to me,
Don't throw plastic,
You can hurt our Earth,
Please help the environment,
And keep the world a happy place,
A safe place,
Listen to me,
We love our world,
It is so cool,
Don't use plastic,
That will go to the sea.

Evie James (7)
Abbey Gate College Infant & Junior School, Aldford

Our Earth

The trees wave in the wind,
The sunshine rises and is very bright,
The rivers and ponds are frozen,
The heron is waiting for the fish,
Dark and light clouds in the sky,
The geese fly to their nests,
Save the world, keep it healthy.

Lydia Barnes (6)
Abbey Gate College Infant & Junior School, Aldford

The Beautiful Reef

I am a fish who lives on the reef,
I'm so happy here, it's beyond belief,

Please help us protect our homes,
Otherwise, we will just be bones,

Please help me or I will die,
Or they will turn me into fish pie!

Archie Chantler (7)
Abbey Gate College Infant & Junior School, Aldford

Save Our Rainforest

Saving this planet is our aim,
Please don't chop too many trees down,
We need to save our rainforests,
This is how we want to be,
Saving Earth is what we like to do,
Without the trees, how would we breathe?

Nerea Morente Lopez (7)
Abbey Gate College Infant & Junior School, Aldford

Mr Myrtle The Turtle

There was once a happy turtle,
Whose name was Mr Myrtle,
He was worried about pollution,
But came up with a solution,
If you use a bag with plastic in,
Make sure you throw it in the bin.

Bertie Chantler (5)
Abbey Gate College Infant & Junior School, Aldford

The Seasons

Spring is coming and bunnies are hopping,
When summer is hot, I like ice cream a lot,
Orange and red leaves fall in autumn,
In winter, Christmas trees twinkle and snow can sprinkle.

Beatrice Bennette (5)
Abbey Gate College Infant & Junior School, Aldford

Our Earth

Butterflies and bees dancing, having fun,
Poppies, roses, and daisies sitting in the sun,
We need nature, it's the world's little feature,

Plastic, packets, bottles, and more,
We don't need this rubbish,
Certainly not on the floor,
Please, please help, not ignore,

You've done enough damage,
We need to stop,
Come on, guys,
It doesn't take a lot,

We can make this a much better place,
Only if we talk about it face-to-face,
We can care for the animals and our home,
And all come together, so we're not alone,

You know this was beautiful before we came,
Look at all this junk,
And now we are the ones to blame,
It's not meant to look like a dump.

Phoebe Adams (10)
Dacre Braithwaite CE (VA) Primary School, Harrogate

Help!

Clouds dance and greet,
Sheep cry while red kites fly,
Rivers splash and crash,
Grass sways and trees play,

Plastic everywhere,
On grass, fields, and roads,
People dropping things
Like they don't even care,

Bottles, packets, and wasted food
Are just there,
Can you not see a bin
Anywhere?

Animals are getting stuck
In food packets
That are left on the floor,
Just pick it up!

Do not litter, please,
It is not hard,
Find a bin,
Do not leave it discarded everywhere,

Try to walk somewhere,
Or ride a bike,
Don't drop litter on the ground,
And don't chop trees down with a saw,

You could rescue animals
To help the population,
Help the world be a better place,
And pick up litter as a whole nation,

Plant more trees,
Come on, everyone, let's make a difference,
Do lots to help,
I have told you what to do,

Pick up litter,
Don't leave it discarded on the floor,
Plant trees, help the wildlife,
Help the world a little bit more.

Scarlett Hotham (10)
Dacre Braithwaite CE (VA) Primary School, Harrogate

Help Save The Earth

Cheekily, the sun smirked,
The dark ruin lurked,
A river was crying,
As it seeped downhill,

Sheep coated in wool,
As they ate, they became full,
The sheep gazed at the sky,
As the sun was blinding them,

Rain heaved on the valley,
Wetting the emerald grass,
As a rainbow appeared,
The rain gently disappeared,

Animals are dying,
Our world is becoming a mess,
Some species are growing less,
But not all hope is lost,

You can stop littering,
Put things in the bin,
Plastic bottles, cigarettes, and tins,
All killing animals, one by one,

We can make a change
To help save creatures,
And give them respect,
Save our planet!

Logan Moore (11)
Dacre Braithwaite CE (VA) Primary School, Harrogate

Our Earth

The blazing sun gleamed with joy,
While ruins were like a broken toy,
Evergreen trees enjoy the gentle draught,

As lazy sheep
Are fast asleep,
A river flows with elegance,
While an owl glides with intelligence,

Endangered wildlife everywhere,
Why do we just not care?
Wrappers, plastic, tin, all around,
Please, just pick it off the ground,

Please recycle, it helps a lot,
Even just one plastic pot,
Just don't drop it, you know it's wrong,
It really does make a smelly pong,

If it's not yours, still pick it up,
Cardboard, bottles, little toy cups,
Litter is horrible, didn't you know?
Come on and help to make it go!

Josh Phillips (11)
Dacre Braithwaite CE (VA) Primary School, Harrogate

Save The Environment

The sun looked down from up above,
Mother sheep cared for their lambs with love,
While the wise old hills stood tall and proud,
And the ruins looked at the sun and scowled.

Wildlife in danger, what to do?
Let's make a good world, all brand new!
Save our small friends 'til the end,
Come on, guys, let's make amends.

Let's protect the world and keep it blue,
Protect the world, that's what we should do,
Trees are being chopped, we should stop,
Please stop going chop, chop, chop!

Reuse what you don't need,
Recycle all your trash,
Try not to buy what you don't want,
So civilisation does not go, *crash!*

Joe Peachey (10)
Dacre Braithwaite CE (VA) Primary School, Harrogate

Help The World

Clouds stared down
At the fast-flowing water,
While the sun grumbled behind the clouds
At the litter on the ground.

Pick it up off the ground!
So we don't perish like a mouse,
Put it in the bin, don't make a mound,
Make it green, not black.

Recycle what you can,
Use less plastic,
And make the world
Beam with glee.

Go on a beach clean
To your nearest ocean,
And help clean up all the mess you made,
So we can keep it clean like a rainbow.

Animals are eating rubbish,
It's our fault they're almost extinct,
Because of us, the world is done
If we don't take action.

Georgie Gill (9)
Dacre Braithwaite CE (VA) Primary School, Harrogate

Our Earth

Green hills stand still and strong,
While emerald trees dance all day long,
Fluffy clouds swaying left to right,
The gleaming sun shining its light,

Fast-flowing rivers splashing about,
Rocks and stones tumbling down,
People walking down brown paths,
Beginning to trip over and laugh,

Endangered wildlife starting to suffer,
Plastic bottles and crisp packets getting tougher,
We need to save a range of species,
Like some that live on the wonderful beaches,

What can we do to save the Earth?
Maybe start to do a litter pick,
On beaches and mountains, it's everywhere,
It's time to do our important bit.

Rosie Newcomb (10)
Dacre Braithwaite CE (VA) Primary School, Harrogate

The Wonderful World

The river cried with laughter,
Creepily, the rain slumped sleepily,
The fluffy clouds rumbled after,
As the sun smiled weakly,

Fast-flowing rocks tumbled down,
The tall mountains stood proud,
Fluorescent-coloured birds glowed around,
The wind howled loudly,

Bottles, plastic bags, and fishing nets
At the beach, in the park, everywhere,
Climate change affecting wildlife and your pets,
People chucking fruit away, such as pears,

Pick up your rubbish, please,
There's no room for it,
So stop it, otherwise,
The world will crumble before us.

Reece Sharples (11)
Dacre Braithwaite CE (VA) Primary School, Harrogate

Help Today

Bunnies hopping in the dales,
Quails doing flips and dares,
Sun smiling in the air,
I like to see this everywhere.

The river's eyes sparkling
At the cloud's crying eyes,
Moles' mounds staring
At the birds as they fly.

Coke cans, crisp packets,
Everywhere I look,
Wildlife in danger,
Turning into strangers.

Fossil fuels in the air,
I can smell them everywhere,
Why don't you help today?
We can make a difference every day.

Don't be bitter,
Don't throw litter,
There's always a bin in sight,
So help our world get better!

Lulu Broadley (11)
Dacre Braithwaite CE (VA) Primary School, Harrogate

The Environment

The rainbow had a cheeky look,
While underneath, there flew a duck,
Then the sun looked happily down
At the busy, bustling town.

Cheekily, the summer sun smirked,
Over the hills and into the fog,
While in a corner, a ruin lurked,
And in a river, croaked a frog.

Soon, the Earth won't exist,
Then the animals will perish!
Soon, the world will turn to a crisp,
And we need some stuff to relish!

Please help the world today,
Or soon our lives will be delayed,
Help the animals out in the wind,
And just remember, the Earth is fragile.

Mekhi Machama (9)
Dacre Braithwaite CE (VA) Primary School, Harrogate

Tundra In Danger

Tundras are melting fast,
And they just won't last,
So stop using carbon,
It belongs in the past.

Snow foxes, polar bears, and hares,
They are all suffering
From disaster, stop and think,
It's not all about you.

Stop burying unused tools,
It's not very cool,
All these animals won't last,
Start helping them, like the past.

You can save their lives, their dreams,
Don't damage the snowy forest and the frosty streams,
The temperature is rising, melting the ice,
So don't burn oil, it's just not nice.

Carter Sunderland (10)
Dacre Braithwaite CE (VA) Primary School, Harrogate

Our Earth

Water flowing through the grass,
Two birds racing through the air,
One comes first, the other last,
Little ants chewing on a pear,

But all this joy will go,
Because of all this damage,
It's so bad that we can do this, oh no,
We're going to be extinct,

Do not litter, it's very bad,
Tell everyone, your mums and dads,
Cutting down homes of animals,
Please stop, it's horrible for everyone!

We're destroying the Earth,
A beautiful place,
Bottles, plastic bags, so much dirt,
It's such a disgrace.

Annalise Robinson (9)
Dacre Braithwaite CE (VA) Primary School, Harrogate

Our Earth

Birds fly gracefully by,
Gently whistling their beautiful tunes,
In the shining, diamond-blue sky,
While the glittering sun shines down,

Birds land lightly on the damp branch,
Looking for something to do,
While squirrels scamper by,
Up high into the trees, they go,

Humans have poisoned the Earth,
Chucking everything away,
Rubbish gets into rivers,
Killing everything we know,

Some animals get trapped
In the rubbish humans throw,
Not caring about a single thing,
While species die away.

Jasmine Sharples (11)
Dacre Braithwaite CE (VA) Primary School, Harrogate

Our Earth

When morning was nigh,
Steep hills exchanged sighs,
While the moon was waning,
Narrow rivers were draining

Into the valley,
Where the wolves howled happily,
But some rabbits heard the call,
And bounded up the mountain tall,

They growled and scowled,
While adult wolves protected the ground,
Wolf cubs ran around,
But wise old elders slept safe and sound,

Though, meanwhile,
Forests sometimes set ablaze,
So no wolf packs to be seen,
While the fire's eyes are cruel, cunning, and mean.

Alex Randall De Andres (11)
Dacre Braithwaite CE (VA) Primary School, Harrogate

Look What You Have Done

Little lambs dance and prance,
While the robin plays its sweet melody,
So come on, let's enhance,
Make a difference, everybody!

Bottles, cans, tins, and more,
Our planet is slowly dying,
Gas, carbon, fuels galore,
Come on, am I the only one trying?

Nature, nature everywhere,
We won't have any animals left,
Do you even care?
The world is not at its best.

Pick it up, try using a bin,
What a state we are in,
Recycle and reuse,
You and only you can choose.

Keira Spence (11)
Dacre Braithwaite CE (VA) Primary School, Harrogate

The Environment

The birds are flying,
The worms are hiding,
The frogs are diving,
The water is swaying,

The foxes are hunting,
The mice are being quiet,
The moles are sleeping,

The environment is in trouble,
It might get double,
The animals are getting harmed,
We should be alarmed!

Don't drop litter,
Don't be bitter,
Pick it up now!

These cans are bad,
You can put them in the bin,
You can use them again,
So make the world a better place.

Naomi Gray (10)
Dacre Braithwaite CE (VA) Primary School, Harrogate

Our World In Danger

Damage to the world that we love and know,
By bottles, tins, and plastic sheets,
Animals getting injured right now!
In a lonely alley, people might say they're streets.

Bottles, tins, and plastic sheets,
Damaging trees, bees, and owls,
Struggling through the treacherous streets,
A diesel truck comes past spitting its oil.

You can see the damage around,
Struggling through polluted streets,
Oil leaking into the fresh, clean pond,
Come on, let's just kick it out!

Max Parker (9)
Dacre Braithwaite CE (VA) Primary School, Harrogate

Helping The Environment

Happily, the sun smiled with glee,
A cold windy breeze fell on my face,
All dark, fires, floods, and much more,
Please don't litter, it's the law!

The moon floated calmly,
While the birds slept
In their comfy nest,
Not making a peep.

The light from the moon was really bright,
But the sky was really dark, it gave me a fright,
It's really cold when the sun isn't there,
Behind the clouds, I know it's there.

Ilse Clawson (9)
Dacre Braithwaite CE (VA) Primary School, Harrogate

Help Our World

Emerald-green trees are enjoying the sun.
While happy brown rabbits nibble the grass.
One little lamb is bathing in the sun.

Think before you throw!
People chuck litter in farmers' fields.
They really could not care.

Forests are getting chopped down, homes are being destroyed.
Animals are getting trapped in plastic packets.

Plastic in the sea is harming our seas.
Help our world today
To be a better place.

Faye Braithwaite (10)
Dacre Braithwaite CE (VA) Primary School, Harrogate

The Environment

The fluffy clouds lit up the sky,
As the little bird flew swiftly by,
Sheep on the hillside ran like the wind,
All the goats on the mountainside grinned.

Damage to the world we know,
Bottles, cigarettes, plastic sheets,
It's time, the rubbish has to go,
All the trucks on the road leak.

Hurry, hurry, pick it up!
Do not litter anywhere,
Crisp packets, plastic cups,
Everyone needs to care.

Hannah Ryder (11)
Dacre Braithwaite CE (VA) Primary School, Harrogate

The Environment

The tall, green mountain looked cheery,
While the wind blew calmly on the trees,
The rocks looked very weary,
As the sheep ate grass in the breeze.

The world is very damaged,
Because there's lots of pollution,
Throw it all away,
And that is the solution.

Reuse what you're finished with,
Or recycle it away,
Do not buy what you don't need,
And treat the world today!

Oliver Marshall (10)
Dacre Braithwaite CE (VA) Primary School, Harrogate

The Environment

The environment is endangered,
It is helpless in thousands of ways,
Stop being that stranger
That pollutes the waves!

Come on, guys, let's engage,
And make a change,
Chocolate jars, poo bags, and vapes,
No! That's what we hate.

The wind rustles madly,
As the rainbow frowns sadly,
The shattered ruin is heartbroken,
And the valley leans sadly.

Arthur Jackson (9)
Dacre Braithwaite CE (VA) Primary School, Harrogate

Helping The Universe

The world is losing so much care,
There's rubbish on the ground everywhere!
Pick it up, pots and pans,
Let's make the beautiful world spick and span.
Nature, nature, clean, clean, clean,
Mouldy vegetables, peas and beans.
The ocean needs more care,
So stop throwing litter, beware!
Don't throw food around the place,
Litter and cardboard and lots of waste.

Lauren Elaine Dobson (9)
Dacre Braithwaite CE (VA) Primary School, Harrogate

The Earth's Destruction

The cheeky sun smiled
At the fluffy white sheep
Grazing on the grass.

Cigarettes, bottles, plastic bags,
All these rags are harming wildlife,
We must pick every bit up,
There's a bin right there.

Recycle all your waste,
Don't throw it away,
Only buy what you need,
We need to help the environment,
Or the world will die.

Charlie Scruton (8)
Dacre Braithwaite CE (VA) Primary School, Harrogate

Environment

The clouds were overjoyed,
The streams in the sun gleamed,
But the ruins were annoyed,
A rainbow beamed,

The Earth will come to an end,
Everything will be gone,
We need to amend,
All that's left will be none,

Reuse what you've finished off,
Make sure you don't waste,
Reuse an old cloth,
Animals won't be safe.

Sam Peachey (8)
Dacre Braithwaite CE (VA) Primary School, Harrogate

Our Earth

Beautiful bugs and grubs,
In narrow waters and trees,
And don't disrespect cute pigs,
Now let's have good dreams,

Stop littering,
Don't chop down trees,
Stop dropping rubbish,
Now start planting veg and peas,

Start picking up droppings,
Like your shopping
Bags and rags,
And your tags.

Ben Marshall (8)
Dacre Braithwaite CE (VA) Primary School, Harrogate

Untitled

Birds flying through the graceful air
Whilst clouds gleam with enjoyment
Our planet is dying, look what we have done
We need to do something about it
All of us
If we don't do something our planet will die
Please help us
We need you now!

Bruno Broadley (8)
Dacre Braithwaite CE (VA) Primary School, Harrogate

Eco-Friendly

Please don't litter,
And don't hurt the animals,
We live on a planet with food and drink,
You should care about all the sheep, pigs, and cows,
Be an eco-leader,
Or the Earth will be gone in a blink.

Alan Ryder (8)
Dacre Braithwaite CE (VA) Primary School, Harrogate

The Monkey

"I am scared," said the little monkey,
"The farmer has cut down my trees,
Tell me where I should live, please."
"I am petrified," said the little monkey,
"I see a man with a gun,
He is shooting and firing at everyone."
"I am worried," said the little monkey,
"In the distance I see fire,
The flames are getting higher and higher."
"I am nervous," said the little monkey,
"The rain has been falling for days and days,
Everything is being washed away."
"I am anxious," said the little monkey,
"The sun is blazing, I can't stand the heat,
I have looked everywhere but there is nothing to eat."
"I am angry," said the little monkey,
"Help me, I can't stop this on my own!"

Lewis Riggs
Junior King's School, Sturry

This Is Our Home

Bushfires coming, animals stranded,
No homes left, nowhere to hide,
We all know it's happening,
We're just scared to see,
So we will do nothing,
Thinking it will stop,
But it doesn't and we will let it carry on
Until there are no forests left,
Nobody can survive,
Our planet will turn into a barren, polluted, ash-filled site,
The people will pray for it to go back to how it was,
But this is how you made it,
And you were thinking it would be okay,
Thinking it would be fine,
Thinking nothing awful would happen,
But now you're sitting on an ash-filled planet,
With animal carcasses everywhere,
You look, and it's
Silent,
Not a sound made,

It's still the planet it was before,
It's just what you've done to it,
This is our planet,
This is our home,
Is this how you want it to end?

Edie Wise (10)
Junior King's School, Sturry

Environmental Problems

- **E** arth is where we live,
- **N** ot where we litter,
- **V** ery important people are working for a better life for us,
- **I** nclude everybody and be happy together,
- **R** emake our home for everybody,
- **O** vercome our bad side,
- **N** othing is impossible,
- **M** ake it possible
- **E** verything is possible,
- **N** othing can get in our way to save our planet,
- **T** urn on your magic button and help us save our world,
- **A** nything can be real,
- **L** earn to save the environment,

P roblem is smaller than success,
R edo the bad things you have done,
O vercome problems,
B ecome a superhero for yourself,
L earn to make everything better,
E ven if your life is difficult, you can try to be a part of the environment,
M aybe the colourful environment can calm you down.

Felix Zeng (10)
Junior King's School, Sturry

Give, Take, And Return

The view of God,
The view of man.

I give you forests,
You give me dumpsites.

I give you polar bears,
But you bear their skins.

I give you abundance,
You give me waste.

I give you life,
But death is brought back.

The Earth is in danger,
We need a game-changer.

Can't you see all the pollution?
It is not just an illusion.

Don't put litter on the floor,
It makes it look poor.

Please drive an electric car,
It goes just as far.

The Earth is in danger,
We need a game-changer,
So just reduce the danger.

Tofarati Oluyemi (10)
Junior King's School, Sturry

The Earth

The trees sensed the axe hurtling toward them,
"God save us!" they cried.
The rabbits saw the gun,
"Get away! Get away!" they screamed.
The cattle knew a knife awaited,
"Stop this madness!" they mooed.
The grass felt the fire,
"It's the end," they whispered.
The child inhaled the smoke,
"Stop choking me!"
The grand ocean angers at the waste,
"Stop poisoning me!"
Each day, more and more of nature is swallowed by technology,
The child cries and cries,
But nobody will listen...

Benedict Southgate (9)
Junior King's School, Sturry

Is It Really So Hard?

Poachers, they ought to be arrested,
Walking around like they own everything,
Make them stop!
Taking ivory and making carpets out of the lustrous fur
That once belonged to roaring lions and slithering snakes,
Make them stop!
Selling furniture made out of the skin that was once the animals'
Using lions' manes in coats,
Use sheep wool!
Is it really so hard?
Changing food chains, starving animals,
But the poachers still don't own everything,
Nature owns itself and always will,
Just leave it alone!
Is it really so hard?

Santiago Chávez Leroy (10)
Junior King's School, Sturry

Steal

I give you trees, you give me shining axes,
I give you clean skies, you give me factories,
I give you grass to play on, you give me rubbish,
I give you clean seas, you give me plastic,
I give you horses to ride, you give me cars with smoke coming out,
I give you seeds to plant, you give me toxic waste,
I give you animals, but you give me guns,
I give you peace, you give me world war,
I give you animals, a place to stay, to climb the trees and have fun, but you give me bullets, iPads and axes,
And if that isn't enough, you give me climate change.

Can Tenteoglu
Junior King's School, Sturry

Look Around

Look ahead, what do you see?
A speck of grass, a simple tree.

Look above, what do you see?
The birds, they're chatting noisily.

Look down, what can be found?
Worms and insects on the ground.

Look behind you, what can you see?
A trembling rabbit family.

Now turn around in all directions,
All these things in little sections
Aren't as small as they seem.

This world will never die but we all will,
So start to think and stop the kill!

Melody Caruana (10)
Junior King's School, Sturry

Rats, Cats, Trees And Bees

Rats, cats
Cats on rats
Rats on cats and
Cats on rats

Mice, hats
Hats on mice
Mice on hats and
Hats on mice

Trees, trees
Birds on trees
Trees on birds
Birds on trees

Trees, trees
There are no more trees
Please plant
Some more trees

Bees, bees
Are fluffy
They make honey
That is yummy

Bees, bees
Need wildflowers
Plant some more
We have the power!

Jessica Kemp (10)
Junior King's School, Sturry

My Pond

Newts and ducklings swimming in the water,
While I sleepily sit on the wooden chair,
Now and then, you'll see a dragonfly or a bird calmly fly by,
And I'll just say, "Hi."

This is my pond, it is so clean,
No empty cans,
No cooking pans,
No plastic balls,
No bits of walls.
I try to keep my pond so clean,
No rubbish there to be seen.

Zen Higson
Junior King's School, Sturry

Nature

Birds will come and go,
In the summer and winter,
They're searching for food
In trees, fruits, grapes, oranges,
Babies and newborns
Try to fly with their parents,
Dancing in circles all around,
Twittering above our heads.

Now that autumn is there,
Birds will go away
To hotter places,
Their babies with them,
Now the coldness is here.

Andrea-Marie Rogivue (9)
Junior King's School, Sturry

The Seasons

Mother Nature has her reasons,
For the everchanging seasons,
Winter first and creeping frost,
Flowers gone, the green grass lost,
Spring comes next and daffodils,
Snowdrops bloom across the hills,
Summer's next, the warm winds blow,
The beautiful blooms begin to show,
And then the golden autumn rain,
Heralds the seasons again.

Charlie s'Jacob (9)
Junior King's School, Sturry

Rainforests

Go to the rainforest,
See the blossoms flower now,
Creatures run around,

Nature is here now,
Stars look down on the forest,
Dawn is coming soon,

Rejoice, dawn is here,
Sun rising on the horizon,
Sun speaks out, light is here,

Happiness everywhere,
Light floods the rainforest,
Birds scream loud!

Sacha Dhar (9)
Junior King's School, Sturry

Rainforest

R ivers running rapidly,
A nd animals argue,
I nteresting insects inhabit,
N ew noises noticed,
F riendly frogs fiddle,
O range orangutans occupy,
R epetitive rain refreshes,
E ndangered environment escalates,
S pecial species separate,
T angled treetop terrace.

Lucinda Lapthorn (10)
Junior King's School, Sturry

Ocean
Haiku poetry

Stars quietly watch
As the waves and the seas crash
Upon the beach shore.

Seas hear the rumbles
Of thunder and the lightning
In the sky ahead.

Sun slowly setting
As the waves and seas tumble
In orange and red.

Seagulls are singing,
Gliding there across the sky,
Flapping their white wings.

Marina Piccinin (10)
Junior King's School, Sturry

Tree Notes

I am a tree,
I give you oxygen,
I give you fruit,
I give you beautiful scenery,
But
You cut me down,
You burn my branches,
You set my friends alight,
But I still provide,
But
You can give me siblings,
You can give me water,
You can give me life,
But
Will you?

Dylan Nish Patel (11)
Junior King's School, Sturry

Electric Cars

How good is an electric car?
It's much better for the planet,
I think it can help the Earth, but can it?
For Earth's problems, it could be a solution,
And to our grandkids, it's our contribution,
It's not a lot but it can go far,
So please buy an electric car!

Arthur Norris
Junior King's School, Sturry

Save The Earth

The world is in danger,
We need a climate changer,
We need to save the Earth,
Because it will be worth it,
Imagine the polluted Earth:
No trees, no grass,
Only dirt and rubbish everywhere.
Imagine?
So let's recycle all the rubbish,
Everywhere in the world.

Vera Kuznetsova (10)
Junior King's School, Sturry

Deforestation

Deforestation really is not good,
If you think it's a good thing, do you care about the wood?
I think I hear you say, I need paper for lots of stuff,
I respond, I know that but you should use other things,
32% of all trees cut down now are just for paper.

Rafe Parle (10)
Junior King's School, Sturry

Nature

N ature is our home,
A nimals are struggling,
T rees are home to the insects,
U nderstand how animals feel,
R ainforests are in danger,
E veryone should take part to make a better world.

Isabel Chang
Junior King's School, Sturry

Pollution

Look around you,
What do you see?
A bunch of bad feelings inside me,
The poor old animals right out here,
They have to face the pollution, fear.

Harry Cleaver (9)
Junior King's School, Sturry

Save Our Earth

Earth is the only world we've got,
Until now, trash is all we've brought,
The plastic is harmful like a bag over our heads,
The animals crying and dying, now is the time to put an end,
So they won't be harmed again.

On top of a mountain or under the sea,
There are so many places these creatures can be,
The animals' homes are being destroyed, they need our help,
The animals are upset, it's all our fault, you see,
We're cutting down forests, wrecking their homes,
They're begging for it back, like a newborn looking for a nap.

The nature is our home,
And now we see it go,
The flowers are gone, the bees are so sad,

In autumn, no leaves to fall because the trees are gone,
The trees arched over us like a friend when we were sad,
They clung to the ground, hoping not to be harmed,
Like a newborn baby not wanting to go home,
Nature is everywhere and soon it will be no more.

Have you ever taken time to glance around you,
The world is begging for help, so don't be blind,
You can do something, whether you're big or small,
We can do it all,
We must protect our Earth, we must clean the sea,
We mustn't drop litter, so it can be clean,
Just like you and me, our Earth needs love too,
If we don't act now, our Earth will die,
So now is the time to stand from our zones
And pitch in to help our home!

Sophie McNiece (10)
Markethill Primary School, Armagh

Rainstorm Poem

Tears of rage fall down from the sky,
Blinding me, but no umbrella have I got,
The rain bangs on my head,
I race through the wind like a wild horse running free.

It's like a water fight on a winter morning,
Leaving you as cold as a frozen lake,
I'm imprisoned to the TV, no playing or fun today,
I curl up on the sofa,
But my rainy-day book is useless,
Like an unwanted toy,
It's like boots banging on the floor,
Or something kicking at my door.

The storm is a deafening cackle from a witch,
Calling out in the open,
The droplets are dancers not moving in sync or beat,
It paints the floor like a blank canvas,
Not in colour, but pure water.

I hear someone shouting as the sky frustrates her,
Hitting her empty head, just the thing she wanted,
But suddenly, there's no drum beat, but a huge waterfall,
Tears turn to a flood.

Charlotte Abraham (11)
Markethill Primary School, Armagh

Your Planet

Does anyone really care about me?
Let me show you the evidence and we will see,
You chop down trees left and right,
Leaving the place like a construction site.

I really belong to everyone,
And you're dumping waste on me by the ton,
The fish can no longer live in my sea,
No wonder! It's not pollution-free.

Cars, like factory chimneys, puff out smoke,
And a lot of you think it's a great big joke,
But I am dying before your eyes,
Don't you think it's time you realised?

Global warming is causing me harm,
Do your bit and raise the alarm,
It's time for change, don't you agree?
Let's get together to try and save me!

For all these years, I've served you well,
Providing a place for you to dwell,
It's time for some responsibility,
I'm your planet, please look after me.

Chloe McMullan (11)
Markethill Primary School, Armagh

We Are All Responsible

Instead of polluting,
Pick up your trash,
Put silage wrap in the bin,
Use the lowest-powered tractor capable of the task,
Avoid unnecessary journeys and cultivation passes,
Replace your old muffler,
Stop using petrol-powered lawn and garden equipment,
Prevent run-off from your slurry tank,
Stop burning waste and using wood and coal fires,
Reuse and recycle everything you possibly can,
Compost your lawn clippings,
Reuse old tyres on the silage pit,
Use reusable grocery bags instead of paper or plastic,
Recycle used motor oil and old paint,
Use a refillable water bottle,
Collect rainwater for your garden,
Plant trees instead of cutting them down,
Consider non-fossil fuel sources of energy,
Be responsible for yourself, the planet, and everyone's future.

Samuel Hamilton (10)
Markethill Primary School, Armagh

Environment Poem

E verybody has a job to do, this planet is not just for me and you,
N ature is important, why don't you care? Stop throwing your litter here and there,
V isual clues are all around, man is destroying Earth's crown,
I cebergs are melting like ice cream, warning, warning! This is not a dream!
R ising sea levels are becoming a snare, watch out for the floating polar bear,
O ut of the box, you have to think,
N eed to reduce, reuse, and recycle to bring it back from the brink,
M other Nature needs a hand, this is not what she had planned,
E ver-changing seasons, the weather patterns have no rhyme or reason,
N ow is the time for action, to the planet's current state.
T omorrow is too late!

Grace Curry (10)
Markethill Primary School, Armagh

Terrible Torrent

A torrent roars, sweeping across towns and cities,
With clouds dark as the night sky, it batters rooftops,
It bangs on windows like lost souls crying,
It screeches like a banshee and whistles through trees.

Children huddle together, swathed in blankets, wolves in a den,
It gets worse, bellowing like a lion,
It unsettles puddles, rippling like waves,
Joined with wind, it is an army of nature,
Destructive and nourishing, it is life itself.

Then, when you get out of bed in the morning,
Everything is dripping as you sleepily stumble like a newborn deer,
Small lakes adorn the street,
Sparkling sapphires in the morning sun,
Finally, the canopy of clouds lifts,
And all creatures breathe a sigh of relief.

James Barnard (11)
Markethill Primary School, Armagh

A Showering Night

The shower of rain
Hitting my shoulder, bullying me,
It slaps as strong as a tiger,
Hunting you down,
It batters me, leaving bruises.

It slaps your face
In the windy weather,
Bouncing on your skin,
A bunny jumping through the long grass,
The rain is a strong bear
Attacking your bare skin.

It's crying like a waterfall in the forest,
It beats your skin
Like a crocodile chomping you down,
It bounces into a stream of water
With a splash,
It's slowly filling up the roads, making a flood.

The rain on the ground creates puddles,
It is as powerful as a strike of lightning,
The car windows are covered in raindrops.

Imogen Henry (11)
Markethill Primary School, Armagh

Pollution Kills

Cars contaminating our air,
Filling our lungs with smoke and smog,
Cough! Cough!
The sirens of the ambulance echo,
Gasping for breath, struggling to breathe,
The world seems so small
As it continues to fall.

Forests are dying, habitats ruined,
Nowhere to hide,
Animals wander alone and hungry,
"Oh, please help, I have nowhere to go!"

Plastic fills our seas,
It's like a disease!
Sealions strangled, fish poisoned,
But yet, we continue to spoil our oceans.

So how do we fix this problem?
We need to stop and think,
Reduce, reuse, and recycle,
Because saving our planet is everyone's role.

Leah Wilson (10)
Markethill Primary School, Armagh

Endangered Animals

On the verge of dying,
With family and friends,
Their numbers are falling,
Like dominoes every day.

Day and night, they drop like flies,
Screaming, crying to help them stay,
As one falls, the other does,
As they fall, their habitats fall, every single day.

They are little toys that children like to see,
But really, all of them are dying in danger,
One dies, two die, then all of them die,
They cry and they cry, hoping not to be next,
But that doesn't work, so they try their best.

On the verge of extinction, we need to help them,
Because we need them and they need us!

Zosia Cimochowska (11)
Markethill Primary School, Armagh

Look Around

As I look around me,
all I can see is
the world crumbling right before me!
Terrified tears form in my eyes.
My heart shatters into a million plastic pieces.

As I look around me,
I regret all the times that I should have changed the world
surrounding me.
Seeing the trees ablaze, no one seems phased.
I can barely remember the good times now!

As I look around me,
foxes are fending for survival and safety
and polar bears are sinking below.
I'm warning you all!
Reflect on your habits.
Protect the inhabitants!

Look around you!
Look at the mess you make!
Look!
Look!
Look!

Chloe Callender (11)
Markethill Primary School, Armagh

Climate Change

The winters are warmer,
The summers are wetter,
But what can we do
To make this all better?

Recycle your tins,
Empty your bins,
Pick up your litter,
Don't be a skitter,
And plant some greenery,
To keep our scenery.

Why teach a child to ski in no snow?
They won't have any when they grow!
But to be optimistic, we can save our planet,
We just need to think
Before everything sinks.

If you value this beautiful Earth,
Please start seeing its worth,
To not help would be so unfair,
We love Earth, so start taking care.

Maddison Hill (11)
Markethill Primary School, Armagh

In A Rain Shower

It pitter-patters on the roof,
Like Saint Nicholas and his reindeer,
Out on a walk, it hits your coat,
Like a hailstorm, it's like a meteor shower
All over Planet Earth.

It's as quiet as a baby asleep,
No sound to hear,
It annoys me on a summer day,
Like a bad personality that won't go away,
It yells at you like a monster too.

It plays with you 'til you can't take it no more,
Like a cat that won't stop playing around,
So rain, rain, go with pain,
'Cause I don't wanna see your face again.

Eadie Downard (11)
Markethill Primary School, Armagh

Planet Earth

P eople do their best to help our planet,
L and and sea creatures are growing in danger,
A nd we need to do something about it,
N ext we recycle our trash and tin cans,
E veryone needs to take part to save our planet,
T o this day, we all try to save Earth,

E ach day, I'll do something to help save our Earth,
A lways recycle your bottles and cans,
R educe, reuse, and recycle your plastic,
T rash in the water makes sea creatures suffer,
H elp for animals is all we need.

Alice McConnell (10)
Markethill Primary School, Armagh

Trees

Look around and see the trees,
As they gently blow in the summer breeze,
They come in sizes large and small,
With leaves so green and leaves that fall.

The birds can perch on branches high,
As raindrops fall down from the sky,
They take the poison from the air,
And give us air that's clean and fair.

The sheep can shelter from the storm,
And hide away from any harm,
And when they die and are no good,
We still can chop them up for wood.

So, next time that you see a tree,
Remember what you heard from me.

Daniel Coalter (11)
Markethill Primary School, Armagh

Trees

The trees sway like a small gentle breeze,
As the sun comes up and your eyes start to seize,
The trees are as smooth as a baby's palm,
And the bark is as dark as a cold winter's night,

And the trees are as majestic as can be,
As the tree expands its long, flowing branches,
The trees are as big and tall as the sky can take,
And the trees are as strong as a rock stomping on you,

As the rain falls on the trees,
A new tree starts to assemble,
Now the rain has made a flood,
Oh no, this can't be good.

Alfie Hartley (10)
Markethill Primary School, Armagh

In The Bucketing Rain

The rain buckets
As heavily as a dumbell
Falling on your foot,
A concrete wall ruining your fun,
It's a horror,
Pouring down on you.

It yells as loudly
As a foghorn
Warning you to move,
It's a baby screeching
All night long,
A meltdown,
Filling up the sky.

When you drive through the rain,
It bangs on your windscreen
Like a little bird flying,
Heading for the glass,
It follows me everywhere,
Like a ghost, haunting,
All night long.

Anna McMullan (10)
Markethill Primary School, Armagh

Be Responsible, Go Green

We are responsible
For toxic air, water, and soil,
This is our planet,
For what do we toil?

27,000 trees are cut down each day,
Carbon dioxide just wasted away,
Mammals are choking on plastics we use,
We can recycle these safely, there is no excuse.

Emissions from our traffic,
Our air is not clean,
Change to electric,
To keep our world green.

So let's do our best for our world,
And go green!
It won't take that long
For accomplishments to be seen.

Sophie Gillow (10)
Markethill Primary School, Armagh

Our Earth

The future animal kingdom
Will be like a fire,
Burnt like wood,
As we kill animals.

The animals on our Earth,
Are decreasing as fast as a bullet,
The world will cry like a child,
If there are no animals in the wild.

Scientists are panicking
About a global problem,
Global warming, they call it,
But that's fake news.

God has a plan,
He controls our world,
The animals will be safe as houses,
If we all do our bit.

Harry Black (11)
Markethill Primary School, Armagh

Unpredictable Rain

The rain is like a story,
Or a cliff-hanger,
You'll never know
What's coming next.

At first, it was light,
And then it was not,
Like a candle
Flickering in the wind.

She smiles down,
Sweetly showering
On the ground below.

He thunders down cheekily,
Spitting at us all.

It pops up like a jack-in-a-box,
And disappears like a wizard.

It's like a feather,
Or as heavy as a dumbell.

Joy Dixon (11)
Markethill Primary School, Armagh

Environment

E arth is the planet we live on,
N ever abuse our world,
V ery often, people fly-tip,
I nstead of recycling,
R euse and reduce our rubbish,
O therwise, climate change will get worse,
N ature is good for mental health,
M en, women, and children must come together,
E veryone has a duty,
N ot to kill our Earth,
T ogether we can save our environment.

Evie McMullan (10)
Markethill Primary School, Armagh

The Rainstorm

The rainstorm makes school feel like a prison,
The sounds of laughing, playing, and watching movies,
I hate when it rains, so they say,

The streets are like a swimming pool,
The horrific rain jumps up and down,
It dances through the sky,
Faster than a shooting star,

The rain is heavier than a brick,
Clearer than a sheet,
As the rain dances through the sky,
And jumps off the roof.

Zoe Shaw (10)
Markethill Primary School, Armagh

Rain Falls

The rain falls on me
Like a leaf in autumn,
Leaving the tree shivering,
Banging on my roof
Louder than a car's horn
When it's in traffic.

The rain ripping the stones
Out of the pothole,
The rain falls on me,
An archer's arrow,
And I'm the target,
It runs down the field,
Flooding the peaceful roads.

Jackson Clarke (10)
Markethill Primary School, Armagh

The Animal Underpass

Animals run and play,
On the road, they stray,
The danger, they don't know,
But under a car, they could go.
The answer came to me,
An animal underpass, you see,
Could save the animals, like foxes, rabbits, toads, and cats,
It would take them safely home to their habitats.
In a tunnel, under the road,
Leading them to a safe abode.

Henry McCrum (10)
Markethill Primary School, Armagh

Spring And Winter

The snow covered the Earth like carpet,
The trees as big as giants,
The bushes were cold pillows,
The last snowman waved its hand,
All changed... now it was spring,
The lilacs were pretty as can be,
Birds carried spring on their wings,
Narcissus, tulip, forget-me-not flowers,
All colours of the rainbow.

Mary
Markethill Primary School, Armagh

The Ocean

Dear old friend, I wish I could see you more,
Whatever life holds, all my troubles you can cure,

Watching your waves gently rocking upon the golden sand,
You're like a friend carefully holding my hand,

So peaceful and quiet, so soothing and calm,
All just part of your welcoming charm,

The mysteries you keep inside your depths, the homes you make for the creatures of the sea,
Oh, how I wish a part of it all I could be,

I stand, trying to count your many wondrous colours of blues, greens, and shimmering gold reflected from the sun,
But for now, I must go, as always, it has been fun,

Dear old friend, how long has it been?
Your once-beautiful colours, so clean and pristine,

Are now quite different, something has changed,
You seem outraged,

I can see the rubbish weighing you down,
As I stand here, confused, with a frown,

How can people be so mean and treat you this way?
Now your waves, once gently rocking, are taken down to just a sway,

Dirty and polluted, I can only imagine the poor homes of the creatures of the sea you protect,
Can't people see their effect?

I'm sorry, old friend,
But this cannot be the end,

What can we do to save you?
Give us a clue,

Now I see you're trying to show us, if only we'd listen,
As you push the waste upon the shore, returning what should not have been given,

This needs to stop and your beauty restored,
We all need to help so you can be cured.

Bella Keegan-Devey (10)
St Gabriel's CE Academy, Houlton

The Sea's Song

A light, a reflecting light from the sea's surface,
See the gulls fly free beyond the silver faces,
Splash around in rock pools full of marine life,
Hear the laughter of your friends as you run along the golden, grainy sand,
Feel the blazing sun press on your water-beaded skin,
Dance around in the cool, vast, sapphire landscape,
Watch the summer sun set and rise, the blurry heatwaves giving an aesthetic feel,
As you glide your hand gracefully across my glittering skin, I embrace your joyful presence,
But it won't last long...

Beyond what you see is a dying sea,
I've lived so long, I can't leave already,
I let you enjoy as I endure the pain of your doing,
Spluttering every second, I choke on your waste,
You can help, stop the death of the once-thriving sea,
Your kaleidoscope eyes have been fooled by my murky depths,

Although you can't turn back time, you could fix your crime,
Sea turtles are strangled under my watchful eye,
No matter how hard I try, they die,
Polar bear cubs drown in my deep, dark body...

You can help bring back the light,
It can't just be done in one night,
It takes a lifetime of eternal might!

Grace Bunker (11)
St Gabriel's CE Academy, Houlton

The Mystical Waves

Blazed with all the colours of the rainbow,
A kaleidoscope of sea creatures swim gracefully
As they touch the surface,
Glittered with a million sapphires, emeralds, and diamonds.
The springtime breeze rushes past,
Making the waves lap over the blazing sand and sizzle.
The waves dance in the sunlight,
Making you fall asleep to the sound of the ocean.
Iridescent waves cover the coral and rocks,
Lying on the sides of the bay area and rock pools.

But under the diamonds and colours,
There lies a brutal, fierce, merciless threat:
Plastic.
It makes the waters thunder, crash,
Breaking the beauty of the sea.
The skies become grey, black, dark, inky and murky.
They hide, helpless, underneath the rocks,
Waiting for a saviour.

We must stop.
They die and we are no more.
The pure crystal waves are dead,
Stop the hate and stop the waste,
Make this right.

Maya Arun (10)
St Gabriel's CE Academy, Houlton

Old Friend

S omething needs to be done, our once-beautiful oceans were crystal and home to many sea creatures,
A ll we see now is darkness, despair, and the destruction of this important part of our world,
V iciously people attack the sea, polluting and destroying our sea habitats,
E veryone, you need to do your part and bring life back into the heart of our oceans,

O ur rubbish belongs in a bin, not the sea,
U p your game, be responsible and
R espect our oceans,

O nly we can make a difference, children deserve to live in a clean world with beautiful oceans,
C an you help? It needs all of us to make a change and make the world a better place,
E ven the smallest of things can make
A big change,
N ow,
S ave our oceans!

Izzy Keegan-Devey (10)
St Gabriel's CE Academy, Houlton

Ocean Pollution

Oceans polluted day to day,
Disturbing the creatures' graceful way,
Sunshine looms over a sandy tide,
The glowing area reaches far and wide,
The seaweed floats, it twists and twines,
The fish are moaning, the coast, it whines,
The waves are roaring, their depths are clear,
The sea will suffer, at last, it's here,
The droplets feel a shiver of warmth,
The sea of destruction, the crash of a storm,
A million diamonds make up our sea,
The sea will be happy if you help, like me,
The bubbles rise, they float, they dive,
The creatures are sad, the waves, they cry,
Here is one favour I ask you, please,
Help save our oceans and seas.

Izzy Campbell-Smyth (11)
St Gabriel's CE Academy, Houlton

Global Warming

G lobal warming is getting worse every day,
L ives are lost,
O h, please stop it and use less heat,
B ehind your heart, I know you want to stop global warming,
A nimals are losing their homes,
L ittle animals don't get to live for long because of global warming,

W e are hurting animals,
A re we really hurting animals if we use less heat?
R escue animals that are being hurt,
M y heart is shocked that we are killing animals,
I n my heart, I know we can do better,
N obody likes global warming because it's burning homes,
G lobal warming stops.

Gerrard Headland (9)
St Gabriel's CE Academy, Houlton

Endangered Pandas

E nvironmentally-friendly minds,
N ature needs pandas,
D reams are short for pandas,
A s pandas eat bamboo, they're healthy,
N ature's children,
G rown-up pandas are better at climbing,
E veryone likes pandas,
R eproduce, or pandas won't live,
E xtremely cute,
D rought is affecting pandas,

P andas need help,
A nyone can protect pandas,
N emises kill pandas,
D anger for pandas,
A ll pandas need life,
S top hunting pandas.

Alex Holbrook (8)
St Gabriel's CE Academy, Houlton

The Ocean's Dance

Waves rippling, crashing, roaring,
Soaring up to greet the birds,
Then crashing and tumbling down
To the vast blanket of blue.

A blanket filled with waste; the waste of humans,
This waste infects the oceans, the seas,
Strangling, killing, starving the layer underneath,
The magical world below, we need to save,
To keep it safe for future days.

Once the oceans are restored, the animals free,
They'll dance, sing, and cry out in glee,
So help the ocean dance again,
But we need to act now until then.

Blossom Kanu (11)
St Gabriel's CE Academy, Houlton

Let The Sea Be Free

The crystal-clear water slid onto the sand and collided around the rocks,
The silver streak of light danced across the water as smooth as silk,
The breeze blew back and the waves sang with the fish,
Splish, splash, splash, next thing you know, the ocean is filled with excitement,
But now,
The dark grey water hardly touches the steaming sand,
No splash, no movement, just pollution,
The ocean can't talk with all the litter disturbing it,
A line of bubbling mist in the setting sun,
Trapped by the black world of the vast ocean.

Simisola Taiwo (11)
St Gabriel's CE Academy, Houlton

Deforestation

D on't cut trees because they contain oxygen,
E co-friendly,
F amilies suffer because we want wood,
O ur community should work together to keep trees,
R escue our planet,
E verybody should help each other to save the planet,
S top cutting trees!
T rees are wonderful,
A nimals live in forests,
T he Earth is something we were given, we must take care of it,
I ncredible trees,
O ur wonderful Earth,
N o trees, no oxygen.

Mithra Seluakumar (8)
St Gabriel's CE Academy, Houlton

Jewels Of The World

Serenity ripples through the sea,
Seagulls caw from above,
Icy, lush foam speckled with transparent diamonds of glass,
From the vivid bright sunlight zone where humans surf and swim,
To the depths of the midnight zone where creatures share luminescence,
The ocean, a jar of beauty.

But we emptied the jar,
Again, we ruined yet another valuable ecosystem,
We stripped it of its nature, Earth is blind,
We need to preserve the Earth and oceans,
For there are more than seven wonders of the world.

Ella-Rose Jaboro (11)
St Gabriel's CE Academy, Houlton

Sapphire-Blue Will Be True

Vivid lapis water lapped against soulful sand,
Silver streaks of light danced across the waves,
Shimmering shells sank beneath the golden sand,
Jellyfish bounced high through electric currents,
But the sea is not all it seems,
Beneath its beauty,
The dusk gloom waves command maelstroms to strike all,
Pollution inks out and kills the sea,
Turtles are strangled and fish are rangled,
It's not too late,
It won't take one night,
But all the world's eternal might.

William Darby (11)
St Gabriel's CE Academy, Houlton

How To Clean The World

C are about the environment and clean the whole of England,
O ne world to clean, come on, let's clean,
M ake the world clean, everybody,
M agnificent people cleaning the sea and land,
U nite all people to clean all parts of the world,
N ever put litter on the land or in the sea,
I can pick litter from the sea and ground,
T ime to clean the world so much so it is better,
Y ou can clean the whole of the world.

Gadi Kamga (5)
St Gabriel's CE Academy, Houlton

The Sea's Life

The sea is a colourful creation,
The fish swim along the waves,
While coral binds together like a bracelet,
The kelp dances and sways,
Hardly seen from the bays,
Yet, one day, everything was to change,
The fish cry out for help,
But, to their dismay, no one is saved,
This can change,
Reuse and recycle, that's the way,
We can change this,
Plastic reduced, you can help too,
We must try to save lives,
Hope is waiting in the skies.

Sophia Wood (10)
St Gabriel's CE Academy, Houlton

What Am I?

I have very sharp teeth,
I live in the shiny, reflective, smooth ocean,
I have no scales, I have smooth glistening skin,
I eat others of my own kind, that's cannibalism,
Even though I have small eyes, I see well,
Sometimes I'm playful, sometimes I'm not,
I'm very endangered,
Also, I'm the most dangerous type of animal,
Sometimes, other special fish clean my teeth,
What am I?

Answer: A great white shark.

Romola Taiwo (7)
St Gabriel's CE Academy, Houlton

Stop Sea Pollution

S top pollution,
E verybody save the sea,
A nd pick up pollution,

P ollution is bad,
O ceans are filling up with pollution,
L et's save the planet!
L et's stop sea pollution!
U nlucky turtles are dying,
T he sea is dying,
I t's always better when fish are still living,
O ver the sea, there's a lot of pollution,
N ow we can save the seas.

Edward Arnold (9)
St Gabriel's CE Academy, Houlton

Save The World

C are for our amazing environment,
O ne beautiful world to look after,
M ake the world shimmering clean,
M agnificent wildlife that lives around us,
U nite the whole entire world together,
N ever ever put litter on the floor, always put litter in the bin,
I am going to make the biggest difference in the whole world!
T ime for the world to change,
Y ou must look after nature and wildlife.

Anaya Khalsa (6)
St Gabriel's CE Academy, Houlton

Beauty Of The Sea Life

Not blue but turquoise, not clear but crystal-clear,
The sea with vivid colours of blue,
And calm waves,
The sun that shines
Iridescent colours onto the waves,
And the wind that carries itself along,
With the heat of the sun,
And the cold, soothing wind,
Mixing together
To create a feeling of comfort,
Seagulls dancing around
In the beauty of the sea,
As there is so much underwater life
We need to look after.

Colene Twum Ameyaw (11)
St Gabriel's CE Academy, Houlton

The Ocean

Hidden beneath the crystal-clear waves of the ocean,
Iridescent colours of the fish
Swaying gracefully in between the sparkling colours
Of the coral,
As a heatwave struck the cave of awe,
Me and my friends watched the sun,
But it could all change...
In just a few years, if no help is given,
The bottom will be gone,
The kelp will sway no more,
And the fish are going to be poor,
They're dying out,
Can you help?

Adley Ball (11)
St Gabriel's CE Academy, Houlton

Save The World

C are for our environment,
O ne person isn't enough to look after our environment,
M ake our environment clean,
M agnificent world, we need to keep it clean,
U nite the people across the world,
N ever litter, you will hurt our precious animals,
I can make the world a special place,
T ime to clean the environment so it is special around the world,
Y ou can save the world.

Rae Phillips (5)
St Gabriel's CE Academy, Houlton

Crystal Sea

The sea of crystal,
Full of fish which are mystical,
The sandy beach, long and wide,
Seaweed being carried by the tide,
Turquoise ocean, emerald surface,
Above the water, the sun's a furnace.

But underwater, not everything's great,
But maybe it's not too late,
Litter swimming through the sea,
It's not only affecting me,
This is caused by global warming,
This is your first warning.

Riley O'Leary (11)
St Gabriel's CE Academy, Houlton

Deforestation

D on't cut down trees,
E co helpers,
F orests have amazing animals,
O n the trees, there is lots of life,
R estores our breath,
E nvironmentally friendly,
S ave the trees,
T rees help everyone,
A mazing producers,
T rees are the lungs of the world,
I ncredible air makers,
O ffensive to cut them down,
N ation helpers.

Asa Jenner (9)
St Gabriel's CE Academy, Houlton

Help Tigers

H elp tigers, their habitat is dying because of us,
E veryone, do you want tigers to be dead?
L ove tigers, please,
P lease save tigers,

T he planet needs tigers to live,
I need tigers, so do you,
G enerations of tigers will be no more,
E veryone, save tigers,
R eally, I love tigers, I want them to live forever,
S o save tigers forever!

Reevan Gill (9)
St Gabriel's CE Academy, Houlton

Water

The shimmering blue water
Has amazing creatures we never saw before,
As the icy-cold water
Grabbed the soothing sand
And bumpy shells,
Like a bed sheet blown in the wind,
But the layer underneath
Was calm and quiet,
But that beautiful water is disappearing,
Turtles eating plastic bags, thinking they are jellyfish,
Rubbish flows in the waves,
As we sit and watch it kill sea life.

Tymon Orbik (10)
St Gabriel's CE Academy, Houlton

Make A Change

C are for our lovely animals,
O ne lovely world to look after,
M ake the world happy and clean,
M agnificent world needs help by keeping clean,
U nite everyone,
N ever ever litter, you are hurting the animals,
I can stop people from littering,
T ime for the world to shimmer and shine,
Y ou can make the animals happy if you stop littering.

Brooklyn Forrest (6)
St Gabriel's CE Academy, Houlton

Who Am I?

My ancestors walked on land,
One of our species isn't endangered,
I'm a part of nature,
Please save me,
You should protect me,
I'm being hunted even though I'm very important,
My heart weighs as much as a car,
I could be extinct if you carry on,
My tongue weighs as much as an elephant,
I support the Earth, so you should help me.

Answer: A whale.

Varun Premkumar (7)
St Gabriel's CE Academy, Houlton

Global Warming

G round smashing,
L ove fading,
O xygen going,
B reathtaking,
A nimals suffering,
L ight going,

W ater disappearing like a drought,
A ir injuring,
R escue animals from global warming,
M ega to bring destruction,
I ce breaking and water levels rising,
N utrients,
G rass snatcher.

Leo Dixon (9)
St Gabriel's CE Academy, Houlton

Save The Polar Bears

P olar bears will be extinct soon,
O ut hunting for seals,
L ove the polar bears,
A ll the ice is melting,
R unning on the ice, never slipping over,

B e careful of the polar bears,
E ating carcasses because seals are dying too,
A ll of the pollution is melting the ice,
R eally suffering,
S ave the polar bears!

Georgia Nicholls (7)
St Gabriel's CE Academy, Houlton

Animals

Animals are dying because of people cutting down trees,
You're kicking animals out of their homes,
Animals are going to be extinct if you keep cutting down trees,
Stop cutting down trees,
Animals are suffering because you're hurting them,
Trees give oxygen, they help you stay alive,
That's why you shouldn't cut down trees,
You can help, you can do it if you tell people.

Poppy Small-Mercier (9)
St Gabriel's CE Academy, Houlton

Save The Polar Bears

P rotect polar bears,
O n the ice, hunting for seals that won't be there,
L oss of what they need,
A ll the polar bears need help,
R eally hard for them,

B uy electric cars and don't take too many plane journeys,
E ating seals,
A ll the ice is going away,
R eally suffering,
S uch a disaster.

Alice Nuttall (7)
St Gabriel's CE Academy, Houlton

Save The World

C are for all of the animals and our environment,
O ne world to look after and one world to be clean,
M ake the world clean, come on everybody, let's clean more,
M agnificent oceans need saving,
U nite,
N ever ever put litter on the floor,
I look after animals,
T ime to go to school,
Y ou can go to the shop.

Mivaan Gupta (5)
St Gabriel's CE Academy, Houlton

Save The Polar Bears

P olar bears are quickly dying,
O ther polar bears swim with strong legs,
L ooking for food,
A t summer, don't let polar bears overheat,
R unning with their paws,

B ears,
E ating food,
A t winter, polar bears have food,
R ushing with their paws,
S uper polar bears that are strong swimmers.

Eliana Prasannakumar (6)
St Gabriel's CE Academy, Houlton

Community Saves The Day

C are for our lovely environment,
O ne beautiful world to protect and love,
M ake a sparkly and clean world,
M agnificent oceans need saving,
U nite the people around you,
N ever ever litter, you are hurting the animals,
I can be an eco-warrior,
T ime to tidy up,
Y ou must look after the wildlife!

Krishna Pathak (6)
St Gabriel's CE Academy, Houlton

What Am I?

A kennings poem

Animal murderer,
Carbon producer,
Earth destroyer,
Life killer,
Oxygen extinguisher,
Plastic helper,
Shelter destroyer,
Tree chopper,
Pollution helper.

Beauty bringer,
Leaf litterer,
Comfort creator,
Food giver,
Shelter provider,
Life-giver,
Oxygen provider,
Animal producer,
Pollution extinguisher.

Lauren Smith (10)
St Gabriel's CE Academy, Houlton

Change The World

C are for our environment and our sea animals,
O ne world to live in,
M ake the world better and beautiful,
M agnificent world needs to be clean and pretty,
U nite all the people together,
N ever ever litter on the floor,
I am an eco-warrior,
T ime to tidy the world,
Y ou can save the world.

Tosia Surowiecka (5)
St Gabriel's CE Academy, Houlton

Make A Change

C are about the world and the animals,
O ne lovely world to look after,
M ake the world a better and cleaner place,
M agnificent world to have,
U nite the people together,
N ever ever throw litter,
I will make the world a better place,
T ime to tidy the world,
Y ou can make the world tidy.

Jack Kallmeier (6)
St Gabriel's CE Academy, Houlton

Animals

A mazing creatures die because of us,
N esting on trees we cut down,
I n danger because we destroy their homes,
M agnificent animals want to live but we stop them,
A nimals are scared and worried because we hurt them,
L iving creatures suffer, would you be scared if someone took your home?
S top hurting animals!

Ariyan Gill (9)
St Gabriel's CE Academy, Houlton

Save The Polar Bears

P olar bears are going to be extinct,
O utside, they live,
L iving on the ice,
A ll the ice is going because of pollution,
R eally suffering,

B lack skin,
E ating fish,
A rctic guide,
R eally need food, they're losing food,
S uffering without food like seals and fish.

Isobel Foster (6)
St Gabriel's CE Academy, Houlton

Save The World

C are for our precious environment,
O ne lovely world to look after,
M ake the world a better place to live in,
M agnificent place to be in,
U nite all the people around you,
N ever ever litter,
I can look after the world,
T ime to make the world happy,
Y ou can make the world very happy.

Kinza Razaq (5)
St Gabriel's CE Academy, Houlton

Community Saves The Day

C are for our environment and animals,
O ne whole world to look after,
M ake the world happy,
M agnificent oceans to look after,
U nite the world and people together,
N ever ever litter because you are hurting the animals,
I can go to school,
T ime to save the day,
Y ou can save the day!

Sofia Grievson-Alvarez (5)
St Gabriel's CE Academy, Houlton

Save The Polar Bears

P olar bears are quickly dying,
O n the ice, polar bears wander off,
L oss of sea ice,
A ll the ice is melting,
R eally suffering,

B ears are so cute,
E xtra coldness in the cold water,
A polar bear loves fish,
R escue the polar bears from the melting ice,
S uffering.

Mia Hunjan (6)
St Gabriel's CE Academy, Houlton

The World

C are for our animals and do not litter,
O ne world to look after,
M ake the planet clean and tidy,
M agnificent wildlife to look after,
U nite the people around you,
N ever drop litter on the floor,
I will pick up all the rubbish,
T ime to tidy everything,
Y ou can save the world!

Jiyanshi Shah (6)
St Gabriel's CE Academy, Houlton

All About Community

C are for the wonderful wild animals,
O ne magical world to look after,
M ake the world precious and clean,
M agnificent world to protect,
U nite the world together,
N ever put litter on the floor,
I am going to make a big change,
T ime to tidy up,
Y ou need to clean up!

Anudhya Arroju (5)
St Gabriel's CE Academy, Houlton

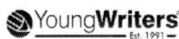

Save The Polar Bears

P olar bears won't live when more
O f the ice will vanish,
L eave Arctic ice alone,
A ll the polar bears need help,
R eally hard for them,

B uild electric planes,
E lectric cars are great,
A rctic ice breaking,
R ush to save them,
S uch a disaster.

Aidan Parry (7)
St Gabriel's CE Academy, Houlton

Wildlife

W e are destroying wildlife,
I n bushes, on trees, in rivers and ponds,
L ife is hard for us, but do you ever think about them?
D etermined to fight back,
L ove wildlife,
I have feelings too, just in a different way,
F oxes, rabbits, birds, sloths too,
E nvironmentally amazing.

Betsy Makinson (9)
St Gabriel's CE Academy, Houlton

Save The Polar Bears

P olar bears are going to be extinct,
O n the ice, they hunt for seals,
L ooking in the water,
A baby eating seals,
R olling in the snow,

B eautiful polar bears,
E ating food,
A ll the ice is going away,
R unning in the snow,
S leeping in the snow.

Neeva Valand (6)
St Gabriel's CE Academy, Houlton

Under The Waves

Crystal-clear salty waves,
A rippling surface of blue,
Covered in a spray of foam,
And hidden by misty blue,
Trees dancing,
As the wind breathes over the sea,
Waves washing over the shore.

Under the waves, lots goes on,
But if we don't help, it could all be gone,
We should help,
And save the kelp.

Benjamin Pitham (11)
St Gabriel's CE Academy, Houlton

Save The Polar Bears

P olar bears are dying,
O ut hunting for seals,
L ove the polar bears,
A ll the ice is melting,
R unning on the ice,

B e careful of the polar bears,
E ating soon,
A ll people be careful and animals fight,
R eally suffering,
S ave the polar bears!

Autumn Griffiths (7)
St Gabriel's CE Academy, Houlton

Community

C are for our amazing animals,
O ne beautiful world we need to look after,
M ake the world happy,
M agnificent plants we need to water,
U nite people to work together,
N ever ever litter,
I will protect our precious animals,
T ime to help nature,
Y ou can help.

Erin Dixon (6)
St Gabriel's CE Academy, Houlton

World's Community

C are about our animals,
O ne world is amazing and lovely,
M ake the environment lovely and safe,
M agnificent sea,
U nite the whole kingdom,
N ever litter the world,
I can clean the environment,
T ime to clean the world, nice and new,
Y ou can save the world.

Isaac Beckett (5)
St Gabriel's CE Academy, Houlton

Save The World

C are for our precious environment,
O ne beautiful world to protect and love,
M ake the beautiful world happy,
M agnificent oceans need saving,
U nite the people together,
N ever litter,
I will look after the animals,
T ime for action,
Y ou can save the world!

Meredith Neal (6)
St Gabriel's CE Academy, Houlton

Make The World Clean

C are for the animals and don't litter our beautiful world,
O ne world, be kind,
M ake the world clean,
M agnificent world is the best,
U nite the people together,
N ever throw litter,
I love the animals,
T ime for a change,
Y ou have to start cleaning.

Sophia Lupu (5)
St Gabriel's CE Academy, Houlton

Community Poem

C are for the environment,
O ne world, always keep it clean,
M ake the world clean,
M agnificent animals like our pets,
U nite the world and help it,
N ever drop litter,
I am being nice to the environment,
T ime to change the world,
Y ou should do the same.

Elisha Gospel (6)
St Gabriel's CE Academy, Houlton

Save The Polar Bears

P rotect polar bears, keep them safe,
O n the ice, they wander,
L ook after the polar bears,
A ll the ice is melting,
R eally suffering,

B eautiful polar bears,
E ating seals,
A mazing polar bears,
R unning in the snow,
S nowy polar bears.

Ashira Muppidi (6)
St Gabriel's CE Academy, Houlton

Save The Polar Bears

P olar bears are dying,
O n the ice, they wander,
L ots of seals in the water,
A ll the ice is melting,
R are polar bears,

B eautiful polar bears,
E ating seals,
A mazing polar bears,
R eally suffering polar bears,
S uper cool polar bears!

Bobbi-Leigh Grimsley (7)
St Gabriel's CE Academy, Houlton

Save The Polar Bears

P aws pinching you all the time,
O ut hunting for seals,
L egs are strong,
A ll the ice is melting,
R unning on the ice,

B ears will die because of us,
E ating seals,
A nimals are fighting,
R eally suffering,
S ome polar bears are dying!

Heath Norton-Carrington (7)
St Gabriel's CE Academy, Houlton

Sea's Poem

Salty sea air and a waft of fresh fish,
A meal on the table with plenty to dish,
Rock lobsters on each plate,
Captured with bait,
While urchins feed on kelp,
You will hear no shriek for help,
Down they fall,
No longer tall,
Nothing there,
Nothing there,
And so then, within a year,
Gone.

Charlotte Mitchell (10)
St Gabriel's CE Academy, Houlton

Our Planet

O ur planet helps us live,
U se our resources responsibly,
R ecycle plastic,

P rotects us,
L ife cycles exist,
A ll humans should stop cutting down trees,
N ature should live,
E xtinct animals shouldn't be real,
T he planet will survive!

Archa Sajith (8)
St Gabriel's CE Academy, Houlton

The World

C are for the nice world,
O ne lovely world to look after,
M ake the world clean,
M agnificent world, get better,
U nite the world with people,
N ever ever litter on the floor,
I can make a huge change,
T ime to clean,
Y ou can make a difference.

Nathan Wilkinson (5)
St Gabriel's CE Academy, Houlton

Sea Kelp

B ig blue waves swaying,
L ong sea for miles,
U nder the sea, kelp was thriving,
E ggs of epic sea creatures,

S waying fish in the ocean,
E merging kelp from the sandy ocean floor,
A nd hidden coral under the kelp forests,
S illy seagulls going quack!

Deacon Marshall (11)
St Gabriel's CE Academy, Houlton

What Community Means To Me

C are for the world,
O ne world, look after it,
M ake the world clean,
M agnificent and clean so the animals can live,
U nite to get better and work,
N ever drop litter,
I want to help,
T ime to help the environment,
Y ou need to help the world.

Orlaith Wallace (5)
St Gabriel's CE Academy, Houlton

The Wildlife

Every day, all my friends get lost or killed,
I hope for an end to this tragedy,
My family got broken up,
I wish to see them again,
Stop killing me and the rest of the animals,
The wildlife is dying,
Help us to stop this,
Protect the wildlife by not killing them,
And eat more fruit and vegetables.

Emily Lay (8)
St Gabriel's CE Academy, Houlton

Save The World

C are for the wonderful animals,
O ne lovely world to look after,
M ake the world sparkling clean,
M agnificent world needs to be clean,
U nite everyone together,
N ever ever litter,
I can make a change,
T ime to go,
Y ou should never litter.

Primrose Restall (5)
St Gabriel's CE Academy, Houlton

Save The Polar Bears

P rotect the polar bears or they will die,
O n the ice, they wander,
L ook after them,
A ll the ice is melting,
R eally suffering,

B lack skin,
E xtra coldness,
A polar bear loves seals to eat,
R eally soft fur,
S uffering.

Jake Howard (7)
St Gabriel's CE Academy, Houlton

What Am I?

I can live in a zoo, not a house,
I live on land, not sea,
I can live in hollow trees when I'm wild,
I am the colour of dark and light,
I am so cuddly and furry,
I am really cute to humans,
I move very slowly in the forest,
I have four legs like other animals.

Answer: A panda.

Lucie Lee (8)
St Gabriel's CE Academy, Houlton

Save The Polar Bears

P olar bears will soon be extinct, so please help,
O ver 700kg,
L oss of sea ice,
A ll the ice is melting,
R are species,

B asic hunter,
E ating seals,
A mazing type of bear,
R eally suffering, help them, please!
S o cute.

Lucas Shotton (7)
St Gabriel's CE Academy, Houlton

Save The Polar Bears

P olar bears are dying,
O n the ice, they wander,
L oss of the sea ice,
A ll the ice is melting,
R eally suffering,

B est sense of smell,
E very day affecting the
A rctic animals,
R eady to catch some seals,
S trong legs.

Aleksander Pooley (7)
St Gabriel's CE Academy, Houlton

Save The Polar Bears

P rotect their babies,
O ver 700kg,
L ying on the chilly cold ice,
A ll the ice is melting,
R eally need your help,

B iting the delicious fish,
E ating yummy seals,
A mazing fur,
R eally warm,
S oon they are going to die!

Poppy Hemphill (7)
St Gabriel's CE Academy, Houlton

Make A Difference

C are for our wonderful environment,
O ne amazing world to live on,
M ake the world spotless,
M agnificent oceans,
U nite the world and people,
N ever litter on the floor,
I am an eco-warrior,
T ime for action,
Y ou can save the world!

Eeshaan Janapareddy (6)
St Gabriel's CE Academy, Houlton

Our Planet

O ur lives matter,
U nder protection, we are,
R ain pours on us,

P lants then grow,
L et us survive,
A nd we will not stand for Earth getting destroyed,
N ow we will protect our planet,
E nd this now,
T he world counts on you.

Esther Ikuomola (9)
St Gabriel's CE Academy, Houlton

I Want To Make A Difference

C are for the environment,
O ne world, look after it!
M ake the world better,
M agnificent animals need help,
U nite the world together,
N ever drop litter!
I never drop litter,
T ime to tidy the world,
Y ou are amazing at tidying.

Harriet Scammell (6)
St Gabriel's CE Academy, Houlton

Save The Polar Bears

P olar bears have black skin,
O ver 700kg,
L iving things keep them alive,
A reas need to be clean,
R espect the polar bears,

B aby polar bears,
E ating seals,
A ll of them need food,
R espect them,
S lippery ice.

Franco James (6)
St Gabriel's CE Academy, Houlton

The Value Of Community

C are for the environment,
O ne world and it can't wait,
M ake lots of friends,
M agnificent people,
U nite, I'm a part of the United Kingdom,
N ever litter again,
I want to help,
T ime to grow up,
Y ou are working hard.

Luna Baulch (5)
St Gabriel's CE Academy, Houlton

What Am I?

A kennings poem

Water rusher,
Shelter creator,
Sun worshipper,
Animal lover,
Space stealer,
Prey hider,
Darkness grabber,
Animal producer,
Storm survivor,
Animal protector,
Light absorber,
Oxygen consumer,
Secret keeper,
Monkey feeder,
Of course, I am a rainforest!

Hannah Goodship (10)
St Gabriel's CE Academy, Houlton

Save The Polar Bears

P rotect them lots and lots,
O ver 700kg,
L ove them,
A ll the ice is melting,
R espect their home,

B eing kind to them,
E ating seals,
A ll the polar bears are dying,
R eally suffering,
S eals are dying.

Sam Huddlestone (7)
St Gabriel's CE Academy, Houlton

Never Litter

C are for your environment,
O ne day will make a difference,
M ake the world clean,
M agnificent world is spotless,
U nite the world,
N ever litter,
I will never litter,
T ime to clean the world,
Y ou can clean the world.

Callan Stead (5)
St Gabriel's CE Academy, Houlton

Save Wildlife

Every day, trees are getting cut down,
Now that really makes me frown,
Millions of plants are being crushed,
Yet no one is making any fuss,
We need to stop deforestation,
Or else this world will become a devastation,
We need to make a change!
So our world can be happy once again.

Zara Kanu (9)
St Gabriel's CE Academy, Houlton

Help The Animals And Humans

H elp the animals and humans,
E verywhere you look is food for animals and humans,
L ove the environment and animals that live all around you,
P eople need to help animals and our Earth,

You need to look after everywhere you live,
And the animals everywhere.

Esther Lay (8)
St Gabriel's CE Academy, Houlton

Community

C are for the planet,
O ne planet that we can live on,
M ake the planet clean as a button,
M agnificent oceans need help,
U nite everyone,
N ever ever litter,
I am an eco-warrior,
T ime to clean,
Y ou have to clean up!

Faizan Nafiz (5)
St Gabriel's CE Academy, Houlton

What Community Means

C are for others,
O ne world, neat and tidy,
M ake things better,
M agnificent flowers and veggies,
U nite by giving food,
N ever litter on the floor,
I pick up litter,
T ime to change now,
Y ou can tidy up the world.

Poppy Munnings (6)
St Gabriel's CE Academy, Houlton

Community

C are about our animals,
O ne beautiful world,
M ake it happy,
M agnificent world to celebrate,
U nite people,
N ever litter, you are hurting the animals,
I can make it even better,
T ime to tidy up,
Y ou must clean.

Sullivan Wedge (5)
St Gabriel's CE Academy, Houlton

Community

C are for the environment,
O ne world, look after it,
M ake things better,
M agnificent animals need help,
U nite everyone together,
N ever drop litter,
I want to help,
T ime to make Houlton clean,
Y ou can help too!

Nash, Sing Hong Li (5), Alfie Howard (5) & Oscar
St Gabriel's CE Academy, Houlton

Make A Change

C are about the environment,
O ne world to look after,
M ake the world a better place,
M ajestic oceans,
U nite all together,
N ever ever litter,
I can make a change,
T ime to get together,
Y ou can save the world!

Arya Shaikh (5)
St Gabriel's CE Academy, Houlton

What Community Means To Me

- **C** are for the world,
- **O** ne of me, nobody like me,
- **M** ake our environment better,
- **M** agnificent world,
- **U** nite and clean,
- **N** ever drop litter,
- **I** can help somebody,
- **T** ime to make our environment clean,
- **Y** ou are the best.

Lucy Franklin (6)
St Gabriel's CE Academy, Houlton

Save The Polar Bears

P olar bears are dying,
O n the ice, they wander,
L oss of the sea ice,
A rctic Circle,
R eally affected,

B eautiful bears,
E ating fish,
A ll the ice is melting,
R eally suffering,
S trong legs.

Kishan Ram (6)
St Gabriel's CE Academy, Houlton

Take Care Of The World

C are for the environment,
O ne world and we are together,
M ake things better,
M agnificent animals,
U nite your family to help,
N ever drop litter,
I want to help,
T ime to make a difference,
Y ou can help.

Vihaan Reddy Marri (6)
St Gabriel's CE Academy, Houlton

Helping Animals Poem

C are for animals,
O ne world, look after it,
M ake it clean,
M agnificent animals are in danger,
U nite and work together,
N ever litter,
I want to help,
T ime to work together,
Y ou have to keep it clean.

Sophie Shotton (5)
St Gabriel's CE Academy, Houlton

Show Community

C are for the environment,
O ne world, look after it,
M ake things better!
M agnificent people,
U nite and work together,
N ever litter,
I want to look after animals,
T ime to help people,
Y ou are amazing.

Edwin Tuton (6)
St Gabriel's CE Academy, Houlton

Save The Animals

Stop all pollution
Because fish in the sea are dying
Because of plastic,
And land animals are trapped,
Trees are getting chopped down,
And they give us air,
If you are doing that,
You are trying to stop your life,
So please stop,
Please protect the Earth.

Jonah Cation (9)
St Gabriel's CE Academy, Houlton

What Am I?

A kennings poem

Water rusher,
Rain consumer,
Secret keeper,
Axe despiser,
Sky invader,
Roof shielder,
Animal producer,
Prey protector,
Camouflage creator,
Darkness grabber,
Sun worshipper,
Light absorber,
Storm survivor,
Of course, I am a rainforest!

Aahan David (10)
St Gabriel's CE Academy, Houlton

What Am I?

A kennings poem

Oxygen giver,
Life maker,
Animal carer,
Food giver,
Plant grower,
Life supporter,
Flood preventer,
Wildlife carer,
Water rusher,
Environment spreader,
Air freshener,
Tree grower,
Carbon dioxide consumer,
Of course, I am a rainforest!

Siddhant Shreyas (10)
St Gabriel's CE Academy, Houlton

Community

C are for the wild animals,
O ne magic world,
M agnificent,
M ake a difference,
U nite the people,
N ever ever litter on the floor,
I am an eco-warrior,
T ime to tidy the world,
Y ou can save the world!

Josiah Uhiara (5)
St Gabriel's CE Academy, Houlton

What Am I?

I am waving but I don't have arms,
I am always drinking but I am not always thirsty,
I am tall and stand strong, up high, and not a windmill,
I tunnel deep underground,
I can see the underground world and the above world,
What am I?

Answer: A tree.

Cassian Gregg (8)
St Gabriel's CE Academy, Houlton

What Am I?

I am grumpy,
I hate land,
I love coral reefs.

I am happy and slimy,
I can go on land and water.

I scratch,
I am ginger,
I wee in a litter box.

I hate rabbits,
I love meat.

Answers: A fish, a frog, a cat, a dog.

Ellie Chrysakis (8)
St Gabriel's CE Academy, Houlton

The Value Of Community

C are for the world,
O ne world we care about,
M ake us good,
M ake us magnificent,
U nite the world and bring it together,
N ever give up,
I do everything new,
T ime to do everything,
Y ou can change.

Logan Gegembauer (6)
St Gabriel's CE Academy, Houlton

What The Value Of Community Means

C are for the environment,
O ne world, we are together,
M ake things better,
M agnificent animals need help,
U nite your world,
N ever drop litter,
I help animals,
T ime to recycle,
Y ou can help too.

Edith Whitley (6)
St Gabriel's CE Academy, Houlton

What Is It?

It is our closest star,
It is bright,
It is a light source,
It lives in the sky,
It is hot like an oven,
It is the colour of fire,
If you step on it, you will die,
It is the heart of the solar system,
What is it?

Answer: The sun.

Emilia Haggerwood (7)
St Gabriel's CE Academy, Houlton

Life And Pollution

L uxurious living,
I ncredible oxygen,
F lowing beauty,
E xcellent animals.

Pollution is killing trees and plants,
You need to stop,
And we have to use solar and wind power,
Protect the planet,
And stop gas things.

Michael Perrier (8)
St Gabriel's CE Academy, Houlton

Look After The Environment

C are for the environment,
O ne world, look after the world,
M aking it
M agnificent,
U nite and work together,
N ever drop litter,
I can do it,
T ime that I pick up litter,
Y ou can do it.

Lucia Mary Keeley (5)
St Gabriel's CE Academy, Houlton

Save The Polar Bears

P olar bears are dying,
O ver 700kg,
L egs long,
A dorable cubs,
R eally suffering,

B lack skin,
E ating fish,
A ll the ice is cold,
R iding the water,
S trong swimmers.

Olivia Miller (6)
St Gabriel's CE Academy, Houlton

What Am I?

When I'm angry, I flash light,
I'm made of water,
I'm all different shapes and sizes,
Sometimes I'm white like snow, but sometimes grey like stones,
I'm fluffy,
I live in the sky,
What am I?

Answer: Clouds.

Antonia Haggerwood (7)
St Gabriel's CE Academy, Houlton

What Am I?

I'm the colour of the leaves in summer,
My habitat is water and land,
People confuse me with another friend,
I'm sometimes found in TV shows,
I freeze in winter and unfreeze in summer,
I'm also slimy.

Answer: A frog.

Isabella Petit (7)
St Gabriel's CE Academy, Houlton

What Am I?

I can jump,
I don't live in the sea,
I love my greens,
I am fluffy,
I have a small tail,
I have shiny teeth,
I like my oranges,
I like to sniff around,
I am sleepy,
I love my cute face.

Answer: A bunny.

Iris Harrison (7)
St Gabriel's CE Academy, Houlton

What Am I?

I'm many different colours and types,
I'm not an animal but I can eat,
Sometimes you pick me up from my bed,
I'm fragile but thorny,
I change in climate,
I help the environment,
What am I?

ˑǝsoɹ ∀ :ɹǝʍsu∀

Imaiya Shaker (8)
St Gabriel's CE Academy, Houlton

Save The Polar Bears

P rotect them now,
O n ice,
L earn to hunt,
A lone on the ice,
R eally in pain,

B ig feet,
E at fish,
A mazing mammals,
R un to eat,
S lippery ice!

Harrison Ellard (6)
St Gabriel's CE Academy, Houlton

What Am I?
A kennings poem

Beauty displayer,
Comfort creator,
Food giver,
Fruit sharer,
Environment spreader,
Life maker,
Oxygen producer,
Plant grower,
Shelter provider,
Secret keeper,
Water rusher,
Of course, I am a rainforest!

Olivia Rossouw (10)
St Gabriel's CE Academy, Houlton

What Is It?

It never goes to the beach because it hates the sea,
Lives in a house,
It mostly eats green food and one red thing,
It is a very, very cute pet,
It is not the colours of the rainbow,
What is it?

Answer: A rabbit.

Mollie Puwar (8)
St Gabriel's CE Academy, Houlton

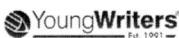

Save The Polar Bears

P olar bears are dying,
O ver 700kg,
L earn to hunt,
A food hunt,
R eally in pain,

B abies grow,
E at seals,
A lone,
R un to eat,
S o hot!

Lyra Tailby-Corcoran (6)
St Gabriel's CE Academy, Houlton

What Am I?

A kennings poem

Deforestation despiser,
Dirt container,
Storm survivor,
Darkness grabber,
Wind winder,
Food provider,
Light absorber,
Water rusher,
Animal carer,
Monkey feeder,
Of course, I am the rainforest!

Caiden Cajic (9)
St Gabriel's CE Academy, Houlton

What Am I?

I am beautiful, bright, and one-of-a-kind,
I am seen in autumn,
I am magnificently rare,
I am wild,
I can't breathe but I am a living thing,
I hate bees,
What am I?

Answer: Cherry blossom.

Arielle Shotade (8)
St Gabriel's CE Academy, Houlton

What Am I?

A kennings poem

Home provider,
Oxygen sharer,
Food producer,
Life saver,
Life changer,
Bird nester,
Camouflage provider,
Sky invader,
Shelter giver,
Fruit maker,
Animal saver,
Of course, I am a tree!

Avishai Muppidi (9)
St Gabriel's CE Academy, Houlton

What Am I?

Half of my tail is white,
My paw is silky and the colour of fire,
I come out at night,
I live in the forest,
I am a carnivore,
I have whiskers,
My nose is as black as coal.

Answer: A fox.

Lincoln Baulch (7)
St Gabriel's CE Academy, Houlton

What Am I?

A kennings poem

Light disperser,
Carbon absorber,
Life provider,
Air purifier,
Creature helper,
Shelter creator,
Vegetation maker,
Fruit bearer,
Animal saver,
Eco aider,
Of course, I am the rainforest!

Yela Talla Kuate (10)
St Gabriel's CE Academy, Houlton

What Am I?

Firstly, you find me on a beach,
I'm not a pet,
I may be pointy,
You probably don't notice me,
I am only one colour,
But there are many colours,
What am I?

Answer: A starfish.

Emily Mitchell (8)
St Gabriel's CE Academy, Houlton

What Am I?

You might find me asleep,
I hide in the coral reef,
I breathe air,
I am a fast swimmer,
You might find me heading for shore,
I dig out of my sandy hole when I hatch.

Answer: A turtle.

Daniel Campbell-Smyth (7)
St Gabriel's CE Academy, Houlton

What Am I?

A kennings poem

Oxygen provider,
Food producer,
Camouflage creator,
Green landscaper,
Sunlight absorber,
Carbon dioxide breather,
Secret taker,
Shelter maker,
Nature giver,
Of course, I am a tree!

Deepshika Gangadhari (9)
St Gabriel's CE Academy, Houlton

What Am I?

A kennings poem

Food giver,
Air maker,
Animal maker,
Warmth maker,
Luxury maker,
Rain protector,
Space taker,
Earth helper,
Nature protector,
Cold invader,
Of course, I am a rainforest!

David Bogdan (10)
St Gabriel's CE Academy, Houlton

Animals

A mazing animals,
N ature's children,
I ncredible animals,
M arvellous trees,
A ctive animals,
L et's help animals,
S top hunting animals!

Darcie Wallace (8)
St Gabriel's CE Academy, Houlton

Our Earth

What am I?
I am round,
I have green, brown, blue,
You live on me,
I'm the third closest to the sun,
I'm the only one that has life on it,
God created me,
Stop polluting me!

George Hillsdon-Crook (9)
St Gabriel's CE Academy, Houlton

The Litter Around Our World

As we grow, our world grows,
But as we throw litter, our world bitters,
As we continue this, our world shatters,
Full of litter, yet no fuss is made of this,
The ocean is overflowing with litter!

Reha Rachaputi (9)
St Gabriel's CE Academy, Houlton

What Am I?

I am a bit rough,
I am hard and bumpy,
I am in the solar system and I am the heart,
I am roasting hot,
I am so bright,
If you come to me, you might die.

Answer: The sun.

Jaya Sunner (7)
St Gabriel's CE Academy, Houlton

Giraffes

G enerous giving,
I ndependent being,
R espect them,
A herbivore,
F unny spots,
F unnier than funny,
E xtremely cute,
S ave them!

Alfred Munnings (9)
St Gabriel's CE Academy, Houlton

The Power Of Plants

P erfect for Planet Earth,
L et us breathe,
A nnihilate pollution,
N ature-friendly air,
T he power of pollution must end,
S top pollution forever.

Prakash Singh (8)
St Gabriel's CE Academy, Houlton

What Am I?

A kennings poem

Leaf rustler,
Home provider,
Life energiser,
Carbon consumer,
Sky invader,
Snow hater,
Honey helper,
Bark scraper,
Camouflage creator,
Of course, I am a tree.

Dillon Harris (10)
St Gabriel's CE Academy, Houlton

Animals

A ctive animals,
N ature, life,
I ncredible,
M ysterious animals,
A mazing,
L oving animals,
S top hurting animals and their homes!

Evelyn Scammell (9)
St Gabriel's CE Academy, Houlton

What Am I?

I live in tree trunks,
I have pointy ears,
I bury my food in the autumn,
I eat nuts,
I have a bushy tail,
I am grey and sometimes orange.

Answer: A squirrel.

Bentley Ball (8)
St Gabriel's CE Academy, Houlton

What Am I?

A kennings poem

Shelter destroyer,
Dream killer,
Food giver,
Pollution producer,
Axe despiser,
Environment murderer,
Tree chopper,
Earth breaker,
Of course, I am deforestation.

Lola Wedge (10)
St Gabriel's CE Academy, Houlton

What Am I?
A kennings poem

Food giver,
Water producer,
Bug shelter,
Carbon dioxide absorber,
Fruit maker,
Axe despiser,
Comfort creator,
Luxury maker,
Of course, I am a rainforest!

Samarth Sriram (10)
St Gabriel's CE Academy, Houlton

What Am I?
A kennings poem

Growth helper,
Oxygen spreader,
Carbon consumer,
Food provider,
Shelter giver,
Nature maker,
Camouflage creator,
Life energiser,
Of course, I am a tree!

Seungjoon Kwak (9)
St Gabriel's CE Academy, Houlton

What Am I?

A kennings poem

Animal home provider,
Leaf rustler,
Oxygen disperser,
Fruit maker,
Light absorber,
Sun worshipper,
Sky invader,
Secret keeper,
Of course, I am a tree!

Nathan Gunda (10)
St Gabriel's CE Academy, Houlton

What Am I?

I have two fins at the top and bottom of me,
I live underwater, maybe at the bottom of the sea,
I am the colour of the sky,
What am I?

Answer: A dolphin.

Amelia Arnold (7)
St Gabriel's CE Academy, Houlton

What Am I?

A kennings poem

Life energiser,
Carbon consumer,
Generation keeper,
Honey helper,
Saw hater,
Wood producer,
Water needed,
Bark scraper,
Of course, I am a tree!

Jaden Kai Tobias Levy (10)
St Gabriel's CE Academy, Houlton

What Am I?

A kennings poem

Plant grower,
Food giver,
Air freshener,
Tree producer,
Life maker,
Water rusher,
Animal carer,
Flood preventer,
Of course, I am a rainforest!

Eric Gegembauer (9)
St Gabriel's CE Academy, Houlton

What Am I?

I have four legs,
I am a wild animal,
I have green eyes,
I am peach and orange,
I have a bushy tail,
I like hunting.

Answer: A fox.

Esmé Beneké-Orr (7)
St Gabriel's CE Academy, Houlton

What Am I?

I move very slowly,
I live in the Milky Way,
I curl like a ball,
I am the colour of grass and the sky,
What am I?

Answer: *The Earth.*

Myles Whitley (8)
St Gabriel's CE Academy, Houlton

What Am I?

A kennings poem

Home creator,
Earth helper,
Oxygen giver,
Shelter producer,
Rain protector,
Prey hider,
Carbon dioxide absorber,
Of course, I am a tree!

Lottie Clack (9)
St Gabriel's CE Academy, Houlton

What Am I?

A kennings poem

Nature killer,
Tree chopper,
Climate changer,
Dream crusher.

Environment helper,
Fruit maker,
Oxygen provider,
Animal giver.

Mia Sunner (10)
St Gabriel's CE Academy, Houlton

What Am I?

A kennings poem

Tree chopper,
Dream crusher,
Nature killer,
Climate changer.

Fruit maker,
Animal giver,
Oxygen provider,
Environment helper.

Katelin McCormick (9)
St Gabriel's CE Academy, Houlton

What Am I?
A kennings poem

Dream crusher,
Climate changer,
Nature killer,
Tree chopper.

Animal giver,
Environment helper,
Fruit maker,
Oxygen provider.

Olivia Ridley (9)
St Gabriel's CE Academy, Houlton

What Am I?

I have four legs,
I have sharp spiky teeth,
I have the colour of fire and marshmallows,
I also hunt,
What am I?

Answer: A fox.

Amelija Tadaraviciute (7)
St Gabriel's CE Academy, Houlton

What Am I?

A kennings poem

Deforestation helper,
Environment killer,
Tree chopper,
Pollution giver,
Dream crusher,
Food destroyer,
Of course, I am deforestation.

James Chute (9)
St Gabriel's CE Academy, Houlton

What Am I?
A kennings poem

Camouflage creator,
Food producer,
Home provider,
Life saver,
Leaf litterer,
Sky invader,
Shelter giver,
Of course, I am a tree!

Ellie Elder (10)
St Gabriel's CE Academy, Houlton

What Am I?

A kennings poem

Secret keeper,
Sun worshipper,
Dream producer,
Home provider,
Life-giver.

Shelter wrecker,
Dream crusher,
Nature killer.

William Elliott (9)
St Gabriel's CE Academy, Houlton

Pollution

Help us stop suffering,
Please help the trees,
You need to stop trees from dying,
So pick up plastic and rubbish,
Please keep the world safe.

Aryan Razaq (8)
St Gabriel's CE Academy, Houlton

Pandas

I eat bamboo,
I hug trees,
I am cute,
I am fluffy,
I live in the rainforest,
If you cut down trees, I get sad,
What am I?

Alva Wedge (8)
St Gabriel's CE Academy, Houlton

What Am I?

I'm fast,
I'm cute,
I have sharp teeth,
I can be black, blonde, white, grey,
I come out at night,
What am I?

Lemuel Osei (8)
St Gabriel's CE Academy, Houlton

What Am I?

I am the colour of fire,
I'm as small as two snails,
I could be extinct soon,
I eat yummy nuts,
What am I?

Frank Tuton (8)
St Gabriel's CE Academy, Houlton

Polar Problems

Ice melting,
Land disintegrating,
Polar regions burning,
Homes splitting,
Habitat destroyed,
Lives taken,

P oison dioxide building,
O cean, stop melting my ice,
L end us food,
A rctic is okay, why not us?
R eaching for my next meal,

B ears dying,
E ffects destroying land,
A ny food is vanishing,
R eality is killing us and you need to help.

Zaki Shihadah (9)
Warcop CE Primary School, Warcop

Weather Around The World

W e are experiencing more weather,
E very day, the weather gets worse,
A nd rain can cause floods,
T sunamis and typhoons are a deluge of water,
H urricanes and earthquakes make the world shake,
E xtreme weather storms,
R ainy days are always to come.

Jessica Murray (9)
Warcop CE Primary School, Warcop

Help The Animals

When it rains with thunder and lightning,
Animals run to the cave,
But it's flooded,
How are they going to survive?
And when it's hot,
They get dehydrated,
They need help with water and food,
So they can live longer,
Now it's our turn to help the world.

Blake Harbage (9)
Warcop CE Primary School, Warcop

Climate Change

When you say three cheers,
You really mean three jeers,
Our world is crumbling,
Our planet is rumbling,
Help it now or live in fear.

The rain bangs on windows
And rivers at night,
And the sun
On the ice melts,
Please help!

Abbie Hauser (8)
Warcop CE Primary School, Warcop

Climate

C luttering climate,
L ingering lavender dying desperately,
I nsolent ivy growing greatly,
M erciful helpers helping lives,
A ggressive excuses,
T eary talking,
E verlasting explanations.

Joseph Harrison (10)
Warcop CE Primary School, Warcop

Wildlife And Litter

Litter is more bitter,
When it is in wildlife,
Wildlife is dying because we are not trying,
Reuse, reduce, recycle by making used things into new,
Help wildlife to restore its happiness,
And try and start a new today.

Evie Heron (8)
Warcop CE Primary School, Warcop

Thunderstorm

When I was walking down the road,
I saw a black cloud and it rained,
Then a thunderstorm flashed,
I hid in a pile of rocks,
Then it flooded,
So I waited for the next day,
And it stopped,
And I went home.

Reid Mchale (8)
Warcop CE Primary School, Warcop

Weather

W orld wrecker,
E lectricity breaker,
A lways getting worse,
T orrential weather,
H abitat destroyer,
E very time an event happens, are we
R eally trying to help?

Jessie Mary Heron (9)
Warcop CE Primary School, Warcop

Weather

Weather is something we can't resist,
Storms are something we are used to,
Tsunamis make the world cry,
Earthquakes make the world shake,
Natural disasters tear the world,
Heatwaves sunburn the Earth.

Charlie Gregg (9)
Warcop CE Primary School, Warcop

The Saving Man

I know someone who can save the world,
I know someone who can put litter in the bin,
I know someone who can help animals,
I know someone who can turn the lights off,
And that someone is me!

Torrin Baker (8)
Warcop CE Primary School, Warcop

Weather

W ind blower,
E xtreme hurricanes,
A nimal killer,
T sunamis flood,
H abitat destroyers,
E arthquakes shake,
R ainy days.

Georgia Lucy Patterson (9)
Warcop CE Primary School, Warcop

Hippos

Hippos are dying,
They're getting killed,
There's no food,
Lives taken,
Please help,
They're reaching and begging for food,
Their homes are destroyed.

Fraser Hogg (8)
Warcop CE Primary School, Warcop

YOUNG WRITERS INFORMATION

We hope you have enjoyed reading this book – and that you will continue to in the coming years.

If you're the parent or family member of an enthusiastic poet or story writer, do visit our website **www.youngwriters.co.uk/subscribe** and sign up to receive news, competitions, writing challenges and tips, activities and much, much more! There's lots to keep budding writers motivated!

If you would like to order further copies of this book, or any of our other titles, then please give us a call or order via your online account.

Young Writers
Remus House
Coltsfoot Drive
Peterborough
PE2 9BF
(01733) 890066
info@youngwriters.co.uk

Join in the conversation!
Tips, news, giveaways and much more!

 YoungWritersUK    YoungWritersCW    youngwriterscw

Scan me to watch The Big Green video!